Otto Erich Deutsch

# Admiral Nelson
# and Joseph Haydn

*Franz Joseph Haydn*
*1732-1809*

*Rear-Admiral Lord Nelson*
*1758-1805*

Edited by Gitta Deutsch, Rudolf Klein
and The Nelson Society

## THE NELSON SOCIETY
2000

Dedicated to Anglo-German
co-operation which made this
publication possible

Illustrations on previous page:
Joseph Haydn, from a portrait by Thomas Hardy 1757-1805
Rear-Admiral Lord Nelson, from a portrait by Heinrich Füger 1800

Originally published in German by Österreichischer Bundesverlag Gesellschaft
m.b.H., Vienna 1982, edited by Gitta Deutsch and Rudolf Klein.

This translation published, with additional editing by Rudolf Klein and
The Nelson Society, 2000.

Printed in England by Springfield Press, Slinfold, West Sussex

ISBN 09537 200 04

# CONTENTS

# Introduction

**Nelson and Haydn**

The Nelson Society was first made aware in 1997 of the unique historical content of Otto Erich Deutsch's book by one of our German members, Thomas Blümel.

The book itself has a remarkable history. It was written in German in Cambridge during the Thirties and the text was translated into English in 1939. However that translation did not survive the war and a second English translation was prepared although wartime conditions prevented its publication at that time. Otto Erich Deutsch died in Vienna in 1967 leaving this surviving English manuscript among his unpublished works. His daughter Gitta, together with Professor Rudolf Klein, a friend and admirer of Deutsch, then co-edited the work which was published in German in 1982 and timed to mark both the 250th anniversary of Haydn's birth and the 75th of Otto Erich Deutsch.

Thomas Blümel traced Otto Erich Deutsch's daughter, Mrs Gitta Holroyd-Reece, and asked her permission by letter and telephone to publish the book in English and arranged to meet her in Vienna. On Thomas's arrival in Vienna in March 1998 he found that she had unfortunately been admitted to hospital, and he was unable to speak to her again before her death a few days later. However one of her last wishes was that the manuscript be given to Thomas for publication. Professor Klein made some revisions to the text and then handed the manuscript to Thomas in return for an undertaking that he would arrange for early publication in a hard cover, with the text and footnotes unabridged.

Thomas offered the manuscript to The Nelson Society in June 1998, subject only to the conditions he had accepted, and the arrangements for a subscriber issue were initiated by David Shannon, our present Vice Chairman. However it is to Tony Dickinson, who put the text on disk, to Sue Morris, with her linguistic abilities, and to Alan Pigott and other committee members past and present who gave support, that so much is owed for their time and devotion to the task of preparing and publishing this work in English.

It is appropriate that publication coincides with the bi-centenary of the homeward journey which it describes, and fills many gaps in our knowledge.

Our special thanks are due to Thomas Blümel for his major contribution towards publication stemming from his original offer of the manuscript to The Nelson Society, and to Professor Rudolf Klein for his part in this scholarly work which will surely become an essential component of any Nelson Library.

Derek Hayes
Chairman of The Nelson Society
Billingshurst, August 2000.

2

# List of Subscribers

Commodore H J P Adams AM RAN (Rtd)
Lt Cdr C P Addis MBE RN
Roger Anderson
Douglas & Sylvia Andrews
Eric C Avery
Mark Barrett
Leslie H Bennett
Joan & Adrian Bridge
E Borgman Brouwer
Jack Cooper
Charles Davis
Dr R A S Dunn
R F Evans
R C Fiske
Margaret-Eleanor Fleuty
Dennis J Gamble
Carole Geddes
Alan R J Girling
Rear Admiral and Mrs Edward Gueritz
Roger Hanlon
Simon Harris
R G Hart MBE
Derek R Hayes
J David Hilton
Robert C James
M R C Jeary
Penelope Kadenaur
Clinton Lee
James M Maps
Patrick Marion
Professor Denis McCaldin

John G McCarthy Jr
Professor Norman McCord
Mr & Mrs B Meaking
L W Merrin
E J Milam
Susan Morris
David Muriss
Michael Nash
Miss Alice Needham
R L Parker
C A Peacock
Joan Yvonne Potton
Ron Reed
Clive Richards OBE
D Rogerson
Patrick J C Ryall
Darryl J Seeby
Ray Sellers
G A B Shufflebotham
R M Smaling
Commodore J B Snow RAN (Rtd)
E & D M Tushingham
Jorge Valezco
Edgar Vincent
G. Ernest Waring
Gary Williams


and 36 anonymous subscribers

# *Foreword*

A chance, minor incident gave rise to this study of an episode in Nelson's life. Some years ago, in the autumn of 1929, I was contacted by the Vienna Broadcasting Station and invited to write an article on Haydn's so-called Nelson Mass at very short notice. The article was to appear in the Radio Programme Magazine introducing the performance of the Mass, which was broadcast soon afterwards from a town in Lower Austria. This small work brought to light a few facts previously unknown, but it also showed that in the vast literature about the great musician and in the still more formidable literature about the great sea hero, the meetings of Nelson and Haydn were still almost unexplored. Gradually more and more documents were found relating to the days spent by Nelson and his beautiful friend Lady Hamilton, in Austria, especially in Vienna and Eisenstadt (which at this time was a town in Hungary). Amongst them were musical works of various kinds, such as the forgotten Nelson Aria by Haydn and the Ode by Miss Knight upon which the aria was based, a Latin and a German poem on Nelson, his portraits painted in Vienna, and a number of other things which were unknown until now. The Nelson literature of a hundred years ago concentrated much more on this episode than later books on Nelson. More recent work has overlooked, obscured and buried the Vienna period under the wealth of later material. It seemed especially important that the numerous new documents should be compared and brought into line with the many facts already known, and worthwhile writing an entire book on those two months of Nelson's life. When I came to England in the summer of 1939, I was able to write this book in Cambridge; here, in the University Library and in the British Museum, I completed the notes brought with me from Vienna.

The book deals with the hero's return to England in leisurely fashion after his first great victory, and staying, almost in a state of inertia, in foreign countries until the fresh wreath of laurels prepared for him in his homeland had faded.

A book about the Nelson who, while longing to frustrate Napoleon's retreat from Egypt, stayed yet another year in the Mediterranean because of Lady Hamilton. Another Samson and Delilah, Rinaldo and Armida, Hercules and Omphale, Anthony and Cleopatra, characters with whom he and she were compared in his own and later times; another Ulysses and Circe (in which role Romney painted Lady Hamilton) or rather Ulysses and Calypso; but Calypso who accompanied the hero she had conquered to his home. Romney also painted Lady Hamilton as a praying nun, and in this attitude - resembling a penitent Magdalen - one willingly forgives her. Just as her friend, Queen Maria Carolina of Naples, found a posthumous defender in Alexander von Helfert, so good natured, romance loving Austria accorded the beautiful sinner an affectionate reception on her way home.

It is a greeting from Old Vienna, which has charmed so many English travellers since the 17th century, a salute to London and to England, which is now returning in full measure to so many Austrians, the hospitality so joyfully given to Nelson and his friends.

Here I would like to express my special thanks to several people who have assisted me in the preparation of this work:   Cecil B. Oldham and the late Edmund van der Straeten in London,  Sander Wolf (formerly of Eisenstadt) and Dr. Andre Csatkai of Oedenburg, Franz Köhler of Vienna, Georg Mayer in London, Franz Artaria and  Alois Trost of Vienna, Dr. Hugo Botstiber and two Viennese collectors, Alois Heymann and Max von Portheim;  some of whom unfortunately have meanwhile passed away.  Lastly, acknowledgements are due to all public collections which are specifically mentioned in the text.

[Otto Erich Deutsch, Cambridge, September 1939]

The first English translation of this book, made by my friend, Percy H. Muir, together with the original 24 illustrations was destroyed in London in 1941.

The revised version was again translated in 1945, the illustrations have been replaced, as far as possible, and a number of new ones added.

I should like to thank especially Mr. D. R. Wakeling for his great help in revising the new English version.

[O. E. D.  Cambridge, January 1946]

# CHAPTER 1
## Sketch of the Political Situation in Europe around 1800

To get a clearer picture of the events with which we are concerned it is necessary to recall the political situation of Europe at the time. At least those events which affected England, Austria and Naples should be brought to mind and to this end a historic review of Napoleon's time will best serve as an introduction.

We are writing of the period between the French Revolution and the Congress of Vienna, that is to say towards the end of the 18th and the beginning of the 19th century, when our hero, Horatio, Viscount Nelson, after his first great victory, was on his leisurely way home. In France the Directory had been

*'The right honourable Lord Nelson', engraving by Richard Earlom, after the painting by Lemuel Abbott, published in 1797. Nelson was at that time Rear-Admiral of the Blue (his flagship is shown bottom left).*

*In April 1797 the veteran reserves departed from the Hofburg (picture by Balthasar Wigand). The war was, however, already lost.*

in authority since 1795 and their desire for conquest, nourished by their internal misery, menaced all Europe. Austria and Prussia having formed a defensive alliance, France in 1792 declared war on the new Emperor, Franz II.

At the beginning of 1793 Louis XVI was executed and in the autumn of the same year Marie Antoinette, the Emperor's aunt, followed her husband to the guillotine. These melancholy events resulted in England, Holland, Spain, Germany and Naples promptly joining the alliance against France. Naples declared war on France in 1794. In April 1795 Prussia and Spain made peace with France in Basle. At the time when the English Minister, William Pitt the Younger, promised subsidies to Austria, the young general Napoleon Buonaparte began his famous campaign in Italy. Like Pope Pius VI and the Papal States a few months earlier, the Kingdom of Naples, ruled by the Bourbon, Ferdinand IV, was compelled in 1797 to secure an armistice and peace in exchange for money and art treasures.

After the conquest of Mantua, Buonaparte advanced towards Vienna and it was then, in 1797, that Haydn's National Hymn for Austria was written on the pattern of God Save the King. The peace preliminaries of Leoben (near Bruck on the Mur in Styria) and the peace of Campoformio, in which Ferdinand IV of Naples had acted as mediator, resulted in a temporary reconciliation between Austria and France. By these negotiations Austria lost Lombardy and the Netherlands, but gained Venetia. In Upper Italy the Cisalpine Republic (Milan etc.) and the Ligurian Republic (Genoa) were founded, both as French protectorates. In February 1798 the French formed yet another Republic, this time the Roman Republic, and the Pope was expelled.

In the spring of the same year Buonaparte set out on his Egyptian campaign with the intention, it seems, of breaking England's supremacy at sea at its most vulnerable point, the Mediterranean. In May the French fleet hoisted sail and left Toulon with 35,000 men. Malta, where the Knights of St. John had dwelt since 1526, was occupied. Sailing on, the French then landed in Egypt and took Alexandria and, after subjugating the Mamelukes, captured Cairo. Following this triumphal progress the great naval battle at Aboukir on the Nile was fought, lasting from 1st to 3rd August 1798, and here Nelson inflicted on Napoleon his first decisive defeat. The French Fleet was almost entirely destroyed by the English, and the army was left with no lines of communication with the homeland. At this juncture Turkey, too, declared war on France.

Buonaparte next turned towards Syria and stormed Jaffa but he found it impossible to force his way into Acre (St. Jean d'Acre) which was defended by the British. Although forced to retreat to Egypt, his army which was left intact after the naval action with the English, inflicted a defeat on the Turks at the same Aboukir.

Meanwhile in Europe the war of the Second Coalition had broken out. Pitt persuaded Austria, Russia, Turkey, Portugal and Naples to form a new alliance against France; Prussia remained neutral. Under the command of the Austrian General Mack, the Neapolitans attempted an invasion of the Roman Republic in 1798, which, however, failed. King Ferdinand IV fled from Naples to Palermo and the continental part of the Two Sicilies was occupied by the French. This region became now the fourth Republic of French creation, the Parthenopeian Republic, and it too was placed under foreign protection (1799-1802). The Grand Duke Ferdinand III of Tuscany was expelled and fled from Florence to Vienna to find shelter with his Habsburg relatives. King Charles Emmanuel IV of Sardinia had to flee from Turin to the Isle of Sardinia, thus losing to France his territory on the mainland. Later, Suvorov, the Russian general, who joined forces with the Austrian commander-in-chief, Melas, liberated three of the four Republics, and Liguria alone remained under foreign domination.

After the victories of Cassano and at the Trebbia in June 1799, Ferdinand IV, aided by Nelson, was able to return from Palermo to Naples, where cruel bloodshed clouded for some time the English admiral's great fame. In June a military alliance between Naples and Austria was negotiated. Suvorov, victorious again at Novi, at the instigation of the Austrian minister Thugut, moved on Switzerland but after an unsuccessful campaign he returned with his army to Russia. An Anglo-Russian army under the Duke of York, the son of George III, was forced to lay down its arms in Alkmar.

On 9th November 1799, Buonaparte, who had returned to Paris from Egypt, effected his coup d'état and became First Consul of a Military Government.

The coalition lost Russia who, under Czar Paul, turned with the Northern Convention against England. Napoleon, after crossing the Great St. Bernard Pass, defeated the Austrians under Melas at Marengo, and on June 14th 1800, he restored the Cisalpine Republic. His General Moreau defeated the Austrians at Hohenlinden on December 3rd and concluded the armistice of Steyr (Upper Austria).

On February 9th 1801 followed the Peace of Lunéville with the result, among others, that the left bank of the Rhine was ceded to France and the Cisalpine and Ligurian Republics were recognised; that Tuscany under the Spanish-Bourbon Louis I, was recognised as the monarchy of Etruria, and put under French supremacy; finally the House of Este lost Modena. Naples concluded the peace of Florence on March 18th. The French evacuated Egypt and their army was brought back on English ships in 1801. Russia, under her new Czar Alexander I, in the same year effected a reconciliation with England. The new Pope, Pius VII, concluded a concordat with France, the Papal States, however, having been reduced in size. In March 1802, after Pitt's resignation, the peace of Amiens between England and France was concluded. Malta, which the English had taken at the end of 1800, was handed back to the Order of the Knights of St. John, and Turkey made her peace with the French Republic.

Napoleon now became President of the Cisalpine Republic, which was then the Italian Republic, and in 1805 the new Emperor Napoleon became King of Italy as well. The Ligurian Republic was annexed to France.

During the war of the Third Coalition, which once again found England, Russia and Austria allied against France, Nelson defeated the combined French and Spanish Fleets in the glorious Battle of Trafalgar. After Napoleon's rehabilitation at Austerlitz, the French Emperor, now in possession of Vienna, decreed from Schönbrunn Castle the dethronement of the House of Bourbon in Naples. There his elder brother Joseph was proclaimed king. Once more the old court had to withdraw to Palermo, as Sicily remained under English protection, where the royal house was defended until 1811. With Joseph's nomination as King of Spain, Murat succeeded him in Naples, while Etruria (Tuscany) was united with France. In 1809, after the war against Prussia and Russia, France was at war with Austria. The Archduke Charles was the first to defeat the Emperor on land after Napoleon's second occupation of Vienna where, again from Schönbrunn Castle, he had reunited the Papal States with France. In April 1810 Napoleon married Marie Louise, the daughter of Franz.

Next followed the unfortunate Napoleonic campaign against Russia, Napoleon's losses in Spain, inflicted by Wellington; and the German War of Liberation, maintained with English subsidies.

At the first Peace of Paris, in May 1814, England was given Malta, the Pope returned to Rome, and King Victor Emmanuel of Sardinia to Turin. The Congress of Vienna decreed among other things on June 8th 1815, that Austria should keep Milan and Venetia; that Malta and the protectorate of the seven

Ionian Islands should go to England; Genoa to Sardinia; Tuscany and Modena should once more become Austrian Dependencies, and that Parma, Piacenza and Guastalla were given to Marie Louise, and the Papal States were reinstated. In Naples however, Murat was to be recognised as King. During Napoleon's Hundred Days, between Elba and St. Helena, Murat declared himself Napoleon's ally and was defeated on May 3rd 1815 by the Austrians at Tolentino. As a result, Ferdinand IV returned to Naples on June 17th (the day before the Battle of Waterloo). Murat, who landed in Calabria on October 1815 in an attempt to regain Naples, was captured and shot. Ferdinand, who again called himself King of the Two Sicilies, ruled Naples until his death in 1825.

# CHAPTER 2
## *The Royal House of Naples*

Naples was united with Sicily under Kings of the House of Bourbon from 1735 to 1860 without a break except for sixteen years between 1799 and 1815. In 1759 the ruling monarch, Charles IV, became King of Spain and assumed the title of Charles III. (He died in 1788). In both countries he introduced administrative reforms, aided by his minister Bernardo Tanucci who, remaining in office until 1777, served also under Charles' son, Ferdinand IV, who ruled from 1759 until 1825. It was the latter who expelled the Jesuits from the Kingdom of the Two Sicilies in 1767. The King was a weakling with a resolute wife, and after Tanucci's fall, Maria Carolina, daughter of Maria Theresa, became the virtual ruler jointly with her minister Sir John Acton, a French born Irish Baronet, until 1811.

Maria Carolina was born in 1752 and married in 1768;[1] she was therefore nearly as young as her younger sister Marie Antoinette when the latter married. Just before her wedding Maria Carolina received written instructions from her mother[2], advice which was to find little application in her future life.

The Empress admonished her daughter to be pious and attached the Canon Anton Bernhard Gürtler, her former father confessor, to her retinue in Naples; she also provided her with a library of her own. Further she advised:

> *Vous ne vous mélerez pas d'affaires qu'autant que le roi le voudra et que vous croieriez pouvoir lui être plus utile qu'un autre. ...S'il veut même vous mettre à part de son règne, vous informer des affaires, vous en parler, vous consulter même, ne le faites jamais paraître, laissez-lui tout l'honneur devant le monde... Vous n'avez pas besoin de favoris ou favorites... S'il a de bons ministres, de bons domestiques, il faut les lui conserver, sans en être jalouse... À Naples on a beaucoup de prédilection pour les Anglais et beaucoup de prévention contre les Français. Gardez-vous d'y entrer, restez neutre et louez ce qui est louable dans toutes les deux nations, qui ont toutes les deux beaucoup de bon. Il vous siérait mal de marquer quelque penchant de plus pour les Anglais, étant unie avec un prince de la maison de Bourbon, et nous étant intimement liés et alliés avec la France..*

" Do not interfere with state affairs except when the King would wish it and when you believe that you could be more useful to him than anyone else... If he should wish you to take part in the Government and informs you about state affairs, if he discusses them with you and asks your advice, then never let anyone guess he is doing so; leave the honour all to him in the eyes of the

*Ferdinand IV, King of Naples, with his wife Maria Carolina and his children. Painting by*
*Angelica Kauffmann (Rome, 1782/3).*

world... You need no favourites among men or women... If he has good
ministers, good servants, you must, without being jealous of them, seek to retain
them for him... In Naples there prevails a great preference for the English and a
great prejudice against the French. Beware of taking sides... Remain neutral,
praise what there is to be praised in both nations, there is much good in both of
them. It would ill befit you to betray an inclination for the English, married as
you are to a prince of the House of Bourbon and we being intimately connected
and allied with France...".

It is true that this wise mother, who died in 1780 could have had as little
foreboding of the French Revolution as of the rise of Napoleon. When the latter
transferred the Kingdom of Naples to his brother in 1805, he described Maria
Carolina as a "criminal woman". She, however, the strongest daughter of that
strong mother, vindicated her sister and the Bourbons, who were already
dethroned in Paris. She represented the natural enemy of the new France and
her new ruler. Maria Carolina is described as intelligent and charming,
vivacious and persevering but, as a wife, not altogether a model of fidelity[3]

Let us now turn to the King of whom we shall hear little in later chapters.
He was a keen hunter and a great lover of music. The composer Cimarosa was
in his "actual service" but despite this was condemned to death because of his
participation in the revolutionary movement of 1799 and only rescued by

intervention[4] from on high. Ferdinand himself was a practical musician and particularly fond of the *lira*, or *Radleier*, a semi-mechanised stringed hurdy-gurdy. Norbert Hadrava, Secretary to the Austrian Legation, who was a skilled player, taught the King the necessary fingering. Hadrava gradually assumed the post of *Maître de Plaisir* at Court, a post which entailed the various duties of providing scores, giving music lessons and arranging concerts. As a consequence of his musical activities at Court, the Legation had to forego his services almost entirely, but under Thugut this was willingly tolerated.[5] In 1785 the King commissioned Haydn in Vienna to write several *concerti* for the *lira*, and, liking them, he ordered others of the same kind in 1790. The first order seems to have comprised five *Concerti* for two *liras*, horns and strings. When he received them, the King considered appointing Haydn to Naples, a project which came to nothing because of Haydn's loyalty to his Patron, Prince Nikolaus I Esterházy. The second commission comprised a number of *Notturni* in three movements for two *liras* with accompaniments for Clarinets, Horns, Violas, Cello and Bass. After Prince Esterházy's death in 1790 the King tried once again to secure Haydn's services.[6] This time however the master's first journey to England was the real or alleged impediment. Haydn personally handed the *Notturni* to the King in Vienna on December 13th 1790, who intended to have them performed two days later as the master was soon to start on his journey. As Haydn had previously promised the King that after Prince Esterházy's death he would accept his appointment, Ferdinand left with reluctance, only to come back an hour later to extract from the master an assurance that he would come to Naples after his return from England. This promise was not to be fulfilled. The King gave Haydn a recommendation to the Neapolitan Ambassador in London, Fabrizio Ruffo Prince Castelcicala[7] , and later had a tobacco box forwarded to him as a gift, which Haydn afterwards preserved in his souvenir cabinet. As virtuosi of the *lira* had become rare even in 1790, Haydn transcribed some of these commissioned compositions for other instruments. He substituted for one *lira* a Flute, an Oboe for the other, and instead of Clarinets he used Violins. In this form Haydn had these works repeatedly performed in the London Salomon Concerts in 1791/92. Some of them were published in this form. Old copies of the *lira* works of Haydn are preserved in the archives of the *Gesellschaft der Musikfreunde* in Vienna.[8] Incidentally, the King commissioned other composers also to write similar works for himself and Hadrava. That the King was occasionally engaged in singing we shall hear later on. A coloured engraving by Bood, a pupil of Bartolozzi, after a painting by Angelica Kauffman, representing the uncomely King in the vast circle of his family, was printed in London in 1790.

1 Ferdinand was first engaged to Maria Carolina's elder sister, Maria Josepha, who had died tragically in 1767 during festivities in Vienna in honour of her and Ferdinand.

2 *Briefe der Kaiserin Maria Theresia an Kinder und Freunde,* edited by Alfred von Arneth, vol. 3 Vienna 1881 pp.32-44. In the English selection (London 1939, pp. 97-110) the letter is shortened.

3 Later accounts of the Queen's immoral life seem to be exaggerated.

4 Cimarosa died in 1801, in consequence, it is said, of the ill treatment. He had composed a revolutionary Hymn (Text by Luigi Rossi).

5 Alexander Freiherr von Helfert, *Zeugenverhör über Maria Carolina... aus der Zeit von der grossen französischen Revolution,* Vienna 1879, p.146. - Franz Maria Freiherr von Thugut, the later Chancellor, was Austria's Ambassador in Naples from 1787 to 1789.

6 Georg August Griesinger, *Biographische Notizen über Haydn,* Leipzig 1810, pp36 and 105

7 He is mentioned in Haydn's diary of 1792 as one of the three Ambassadors, whom he visited or intended to visit in London.

8 New editions by H. C. Robbins Landon, Verlag Doblinger, in the series *Dilette Musicale,* Vienna (Editorial note).

# CHAPTER 3
## *Two Major and Two Minor Characters*

Before we continue this review of the history of Naples as far as it is relevant to our subject, it is necessary that we should now meet two main and two subordinate characters all of whom will play a more important part in this book than the King of Naples. This mere shadow of royalty outlived the real actors of our play in years but none of them in fame.

First of all there is Sir William Hamilton - a foster brother of George III - the elegant and learned English Ambassador, who was frequently to be seen at Ferdinand's hunting parties. He was born in 1730 and took up residence in Naples in 1764. In 1758 he married his first wife, Miss Catherine Barlow, who will play only a minor part in this book. Their only child, a daughter, died at

*Sir William Hamilton, after an engraving by G Morghen. From 1764 Hamilton was Ambassador to the Neapolitan Court.*

the early age of 16. Lady Catherine died in 1782[1] . Sir William played the violin and viola fairly well and was a pupil of Felice de Giardini. The elder Mozart and his children had made his acquaintance in London shortly before his departure for Italy in 1764. In Leopold Mozart's notebook there is an entry, "Mr Hamilton in King's Mews", and an additional note *itzt Gesanter in Neapel* (now Ambassador in Naples)[2], identifies him as our Sir William without doubt. (Hamilton was not knighted until 1772). When Wolfgang Amadeus Mozart and his father visited Naples in 1770, they renewed the acquaintance. The two Mozarts remained there from May 14th until June 25th and during that time they were often guests in the Villa Angelica, Sir William's summer residence in Caserta at the foot of Vesuvius[3]. This time we find in Leopold's travel notes: *L'ambassadore d'Inghilterra e la sua Signora*[4] (The Ambassador of England and his wife.) Mozart senior also wrote to his wife in Salzburg that (the first) Lady Hamilton "plays the piano in a moving manner" and he found her "a very pleasant person"[5]. On May 28th she, with other ladies, arranged the musical party which Wolfgang gave in Naples. In the autumn of the same year Charles Burney, the music historian, visited that city and in his book "The Present State of Music in France and Italy"[6] he mentions Sir William and his wife. Burney visited them on October 26th in their villa where he remained for two or three days. He also tells us that Sir William had two musicians in his service, a violinist and a cellist. On the 29th the Hamiltons gave a grand concert in their town residence in Palazzo Sessa, at which Lady Hamilton showed herself a pianist of outstanding ability. On November 4th Burney joined the Hamiltons in their opera box at St. Carlo, the famous opera house of Naples. On the following day he had lunch in their house where another concert was given in the afternoon and where he stayed until two o'clock in the morning. On that occasion Burney admired Hamilton's Art and Natural History collections[7] where he noticed among other things the so called Venus of Correggio[8] and some Etruscan vases[9]; he visited the library[10] and enjoyed a prolonged discussion about old music, a subject in which Sir William was interested. Sir William's collection of antiquities - of which we shall hear later - was acquired gradually by the British Museum. He had also presented other gifts to the Museum during the years 1772 and 1784, and indeed his collection of vases formed the foundation of the Museum's collections in the Greek and Roman rooms.

Michael Kelly, the Irish singer, who stayed in Naples in 1777/8 wrote in his "Reminiscences" about the private concerts in Hamilton's house and praised Lady Hamilton as Italy's first pianist (undoubtedly Irish blarney). William Beckford, a relative of Sir William's, came to Naples as a young man of twenty and formed a close friendship with Catherine. Nearly sixty years later he related to Cyrus Redding ("Memoir of Beckford", published in 1859): "She was a charming creature, I do not mean 'the Nelson'... an angel of purity. She lived uncorrupted in the midst of the [frivolous] Neapolitan Court... I never saw so

*Sir William Hamilton and his first wife Catherine. Oil painting on copper by David Allan (1770). Vesuvius is in the background.*

heavenly minded a creature. Her power of musical execution was wonderful - so sweetly soft was her touch - she seemed as if she had thrown her own essence into the music. I used to listen to her like one entranced..." In his book "Dreams, Waking Thoughts, and Incidents" (1780 not printed, revised version Italy 1834) Beckford again writes of her: "Lady Hamilton sat down to the pianoforte. No performance I ever heard produced such soothing effects; they seemed the emanations of a pure, uncontaminated mind, at peace with itself and benevolently desirous of diffusing that happy tranquillity around it; these were modes a Grecian legislature would have encouraged to further the triumph over vice of the most amiable nature"[11] . About 1780 Lady Catherine Hamilton is said to have been playing duets with the Abbé Sterkel at the Court of Naples, at that time an unusual form of playing[12] . A minuet, which is preserved in a handwritten collection of Charles Frederick Weidemann (King's Music Library, in the British Museum) seems to have been composed by Catherine herself. She died suddenly on August 27th 1782. Her obituary which appeared in Cramer's

*Emma Hamilton. the second wife of the Neapolitan Ambassador Sir William Hamilton, in one of her 'Attitudes' as the Sibyll. Painting by Elisabeth Vigée-Le Brun, 1792*

*Magazin der Musik* (Hamburg 1783, vol. 1 pp.341 f.) is an appreciation similar to that by Kelly. In 1785 Sir William asked the Music Professor of Naples, Lorenzo Moser, to arrange a number of Handel's Oratorio - songs as string trios; they appeared later in London as 18 "posthumous" Divertimenti. In about 1800 the Austrian composer Adalbert Gyrowetz stayed in Naples for two years; there, he tells us in his autobiography (1848), he had his quartets and orchestral works played at the Hamiltons.

In 1784 the Scot, Sir William Hamilton, met the Welsh woman, Emma Lyon called Harte, in whom we are mostly interested and who is really the centre around which our story revolves. She was born in 1765 and after several adventurous years became the mistress of the Hon. Charles Francis Greville, Sir William's nephew and predetermined heir, who in 1786 arranged for her to go to Naples with her mother[13] to join his uncle. Goethe met them when he arrived in Naples in the Spring of 1787. In his *Italienische Reise* he writes:

> *Caserta, den 16. März 1787 .. Der Ritter Hamilton, der noch immer als englischer Gesandter hier lebt, hat nun, nach so langer Kunstliebhaberei, nach so langem Naturstudium, den Gipfel aller Natur-und Kunstfreude in einem schönen Mädchen gefunden. Er hat sie bei sich, eine Engländerin von etwa 20 Jahren. Sie ist sehr schön*

*und wohlgebaut. Er hat ihr ein griechisches Gewand machen lassen, das sie trefflich kleidet, und dazu löst sie ihre Haare auf, nimmt ein paar Shawls und macht eine Abwechslung von Stellungen, Gebärden, Minen etc., dass man zuletzt wirklich meint, man träume. Man schaut, was so viele tausend Künstler gerne geleistet hätten, hier ganz fertig, in Bewegung und überraschender Abwechslung. Stehend, knieend, sitzend, liegend, ernst, traurig, neckisch, ausschweifend, bussfertig, lockend, drohend, ängstlich etc., eins folgt auf's andere und aus dem andern. Sie weiss zu jedem Ausdruck die Falten des Schleiers zu wählen, zu wechseln, und macht sich hundert Arten von Kopfputz mit den selben Tüchern. Der alte Ritter hält das Licht dazu und hat mit ganzer Seele sich diesem Gegenstand ergeben. Er findet in ihr alle Antiken, alle schönen Profile der sizilianischen Münzen, ja den Belveder'schen Apoll selbst. Soviel ist gewiss, der Spass ist einzig! Wir haben ihn schon zwei Abende genossen. Heute früh malt sie Tischbein.*

"Caserta[14] , the 16th of March, 1787... The chevalier Hamilton, so long resident here as English Ambassador, so long, too, connoisseur and student of Art and Nature, has found their counterpart and acme with exquisite delight in a lovely girl - English, and some twenty years of age. She is exceedingly beautiful and finely built. She wears a Greek garb becoming her to perfection. She then merely loosens her locks, takes a pair of shawls, and effects changes of postures, moods, gestures, mien, and appearance that make one really feel as if one were in some dream. Here is visible complete, and bodied forth in movements of surprising variety, all that so many artists have sought in vain to fix and render. Successively standing, kneeling, seated, reclining, grave, sad, sportive, teasing, abandoned, penitent, alluring, threatening, agonised, etc. One follows the other, and grows out of it. She knows how to choose and shift the simple folds of her kerchief for every expression, and to adjust it into a hundred kinds of headgear. Her elderly knight holds the torches for her performance and is absorbed in his soul's desire. In her he finds the charm of all antiques, the fair profiles on Sicilian coins, the Apollo Belvedere himself[15] . We have already rejoiced in the spectacle for two evenings. Early tomorrow Tischbein paints her."[16]

(This reference is to the half-length portrait of Emma as Sibylla, by Wilhelm Tischbein, preserved in Weimar. This friend and companion of Goethe also painted Emma as Iphigenia and as Andromache parting from Hector, and these two paintings are now in Arolsen, Waldeck, in Germany.)

On May 27th, Goethe, after his return from Sicily to Naples, wrote: *Hamilton und seine Schöne setzten gegen mich ihre Freundlichkeit fort. Ich speiste bei ihnen und gegen Abend produzierte Miss Harte auch ihre musikalischen und melischen Talente...(* " Hamilton and his lovely girl continued to show me friendly attentions. I dined with them and towards evening Miss

*Lady Emma Hamilton in another of her 'Attitudes', which captivated Goethe during his stay in Naples. Painting by George Romney.*

Harte exhibited her musical and lyrical talents...”). Goethe goes on to mention a complicated apparatus, which was no longer in working order, by which the *Kunst-und Mädchenfreund* (Lover of Arts and Maidens) could put lovely Emma in a frame as a tableau vivant[17] and contemplate her in his villa. Two years later the Duchess Amalie of Saxony-Weimar writes to Goethe from Rome: “Miss Hart I have seen as well; surely of her kind she is the most outstanding creature now living on earth”. Goethe’s words about the elderly knight who “holds the torches” were later on to get a deeper significance. His words on the “Lover of the Arts and Maidens”, however, found a parallel, probably unintentionally, in Balzac’s Beatrix: *M. de Faucombe, vieillard de soixante ans, avait épousé une jeune femme, à laquelle il laissait le gouvernement de ses affaires. Il ne s’occupait plus que d’archéologie, une passion ou, pour parler plus correctement, une de ces manies qui aident les vieillards à se croire vivants.*

("Mr de Faucombe, an old man of 60 years, had married a young woman, to whom he left the control of his business affairs. He no longer concerned himself with anything but archaeology, a passion or more accurately one of those obsessions which help old men feel as though they are still alive").

Sir William is himself mentioned in Cramer's *Magazin der Musik* (June 1789, p.16): "Mr Hadrava, Secretary to the Imperial Legation, gives frequent concerts at which the English Ambassador, that passionate lover of music, and of the viola in particular, takes part despite his age." The anonymous traveller's account still refers to the end of 1786. A few years later, in 1792, we find a "W. Hamilton Esq."[18] among the subscribers to the second volume of the collection of Scotch songs, edited by William Napier in London. These were the first of many British folk songs which Haydn arranged with Piano Trio accompaniment.

Let us now touch upon the musical talents of the second Lady Hamilton. In June 1793 she wrote to Greville:[19] "In the evenings I go to her (Maria Carolina) ... Sometimes we sing. Yesterday the King and me sang duets 3 hours. It was but bad.... I study very hard... and I have had all my songs set for the viola, so that Sir William may accompany me, which has pleased him very much, so that we study together." Emma often accompanied herself on a guitar, and the instrument she used around 1800 was exhibited in 1932 at the London Museum. In about 1798 Elizabeth Billington, a singer whom Haydn had met in London in 1791/2, visited the Hamiltons in Naples and sang a cantata there.[20]

Sir William married Emma in 1791 and as she thus became eligible for presentation at Court, he presented her to Queen Marie Antoinette in Paris and later to her sister Queen Maria Carolina in Naples. Shortly afterwards, on January 11th 1792, Lady Harriet Mary Malmesbury wrote to her sister Lady Anna Maria Minto from Naples[21] : "You never saw anything so charming as Lady Hamilton's attitudes. The most graceful statues or pictures do not give you an idea of them. Her dancing the Tarantella is beautiful to a degree". And five years later, on November 6th 1796, Sir Gilbert Elliot, later Lord Minto, who had previously made Nelson's acquaintance in Corsica in 1794[22] and of whom we shall hear repeatedly in this account, wrote to his wife from Naples[23] : "She is the most extraordinary compound I ever beheld. Her person is nothing short of monstrous for its enormity, and is growing every day. She tries hard to think size advantageous to her beauty, but is not easy about it. Her face is beautiful; she is all Nature, and yet all Art; that is to say, her manners are perfectly unpolished, of course very easy, though not with the ease of good breeding, but of a barmaid, excessively good humoured and wishing to please and be admired by all ages and sorts of persons that called in her way; but besides considerable natural understanding, she has acquired, since her marriage, some knowledge of history and of the arts, and one wonders at the application and pains she has taken to make herself what she is. With men her language and conversation are exaggerations of anything I ever heard anywhere; and I was wonderfully struck with these inveterate remains of her origin, though the impression was very much weakened by seeing the other ladies of Naples." But on December 24th

*Lady Emma Hamilton is represented in three different poses in this painting, attributed to the English painter Gavin Hamilton (not related to the Hamiltons).*

Lord Minto adds[24] : "We had the attitudes a night or two ago by candlelight; they come up to my expectations fully, which is saying everything. They set Lady Hamilton in a very different light from any I had seen her in before; nothing about her, neither her conversation, her manners, nor figure announce the very refined taste which she discovers in this performance, besides the extraordinary talent that is necessary for the execution; and besides all this, says Sir Willum, she makes my apple-pies." (Willum was Emma's term of endearment for her husband).

It must be said in parenthesis that Sir William is not to be identified with the Count Hamilton who was a member of the Vienna Masonic Lodge *Aux Trois Canons*, as stated in Richard Koch's booklet *Bruder Mozart*, (Reichenhall 1911, pp. 9 et.seq.). The latter was the son of Johann Andreas Count Hamilton, President of the War Cabinet and Captain of the Life Guards, who died in Vienna in 1738.[25]

By 1797, the year in which Schubert was born and Haydn composed his People's Hymn, Sir William was already quite well known in Vienna as a collector. Count Deym established in the centre of the city an exhibition of casts together with a sort of Panoptikum, which was open to the public (first in the Kohlmarkt, then in the *Stock-im-Eisen-Platz* near St. Stephen's Cathedral, and finally in the *Rotenturm-strasse* near the *Donaukanal).* Some of the wax-works were enlivened by musical boxes for which special music was composed by Mozart and Beethoven. It was the same Count Deym who took Mozart's death mask, now lost, who dropped his title and assumed the bourgeois name of Müller because of a duel, and who married Beethoven's pupil, Josephine Countess Brunswick. A catalogue of the Art Gallery, erected by Müller (written by C.M.A., Vienna 1797) mentions on page 60: "150 Etrurian Vases"[26] described by Hamilton and others, with plates by Tischbein, in "Collection of Engravings from Greek Vases", Naples 1791. Incidentally, on page 66 of the same catalogue a group of wax figures, which is of interest to us, is mentioned: "The Imperial Family en grouppe", including the Queen of Naples with her husband.[27]

The second minor role which we announced at the beginning of this chapter belongs to Miss Ellis Cornelia Knight. After the death of her father, Joseph Knight, Rear-Admiral of the White[28] , in 1775, his widow, Lady Philippina, moved to Italy with Cornelia, who was then about 19 years of age. They first went to Rome and proceeded to Naples in 1785, where they became friendly with Sir William and, soon afterwards, with Emma as well. When her mother died in 1799, Cornelia, who meanwhile had taken up writing and had developed into a sort of Tyrtaea[29], remained in Naples under the patronage of the Hamiltons. On her return to England in 1805 she became companion to Queen Charlotte and later to Princess Charlotte of Wales, a post she held until 1814. After having written various books, particularly on the ancient Romans, she edited, together with others, "Miscellaneous Poems" in 1812, and "Translations of German Hymns and Prayers" (some of which were by Gellert, whom Haydn had also used for a number of songs). After a number of years travelling in Europe she died in Paris in 1837. Her autobiography, edited by J. W. Kaye and which we shall quote repeatedly, did not appear until 1861.

1 Anton Maron, a painter from Vienna, made a portrait of the couple which in 1798 was still in Sir William's possession in Naples. - cf " Sir William Hamilton's Picture Gallery" by Otto Erich Deutsch, "The Burlington Magazine", February 1943.

2 Arthur Schurig, *Leopold Mozart Reiseaufzeichnungen,* Leipzig 1920, p.35.

3 We shall deal with his Vesuvius researches later.

4 Schurig, op. cit. p53.

5 Hers was a Shudi Harpsichord. Vide Georg Kinsky, *Mozart Instrumente, "Acta Musicologica",* Copenhagen 1940, pp.1-21.

6 London 1777, pp.316-324, 341, 345 et.seq. In a more recent edition of excerpts from Burney's book the second Lady Hamilton's portrait is mistaken for the first Lady Hamilton. The same error is made by Baron Roger Portalis, who writes in his monograph on Fragonard (Paris 1889, p.176) that the painter had visited concerts in the house of Sir William, "the happy husband of the beautiful Emma".

7 Part of his collection of geological specimens Sir William had already presented to the British Museum in 1767.

8 Sold ca. 1790 in London through Charles Greville.

9 Sir William sold his first collection of antiquities, begun in 1766, to the British Museum in 1772 for £8,410.

10 "Catalogue of Hamilton's Books, Antiquities, etc." Sale, London, 10th June 1809. In his

*24*

collection there were two books from Vienna: Fischer von Erlach's *Entwurf einer Historischen Architektur* (Leipzig 1775) and Eleonore von Raab's *Catalogue raisonné de la collection de Fossiles* Vienna 1790.

11 Lewis Melville, "The Life and Letters of William Beckford of Fonthill (Author of Vathek)", London 1910, pp. 94 et. seq.

12 Karl Ganzer and Ludwig Kusche: *Vierhändig,* München 1937, p.37. Here again Catherine is called "the beautiful Lady Hamilton".

13 Mary Kidd, called Mrs.Cadogan.

14 North East of Naples, the seat of the King's summer residence.

15 Cf. Walpole's remark to Miss Mary Berry, after Hamilton's second wedding ("Horace Walpole's Correspondence", edited by W.C. Lewis, vol. ii, London 1944, p.349, letter of September 11th 1791): "Sir William Hamilton has actually married the Gallery of Statues."

16 This translation is taken from Walter Sichel's "Emma Lady Hamilton", 3rd edition, London 1907 p.105.

17 The discussion on tableaux vivants in Goethe's *Wahlverwandtschaften* has been inspired by the *Pantomimische Stellungen* of Henriette Hendel-Schütz, who had derived them from Lady Hamilton's "Attitudes".

18 In the diary of his second sojourn in England, in 1794, about June, Haydn makes a note of an address: "Mr Hamilton, Rodney Place, Cleston [*recte* Clifton] Hill near Bristol". This, however, was not Sir William.

19 Walter Sichel, "Emma Lady Hamilton", p.155.

20 At least two works of Haydn had been reprinted in Naples in ca. 1790. "The Seven Last Words of the Redeemer on the Cross", in the orchestral version, and the String Quintet "Echo", on the title page of which the publisher Marescalchi shows the performance of the first Trio with the Echo of the *"Altra Camera"* in the surroundings of Naples.

21 "Life and Letters of Sir Gilbert Elliot, First Earl of Minto, from 1751 to 1806...edited by his great niece, the Countess [Nina] of Minto", London 1874, I.408.

22 Sir Gilbert Elliot was England's High Commissioner for Corsica from 1794 and there he was subsequently nominated Viceroy; he was made Baron Minto in 1797 and became Viscount Melgund and Earl of Minto in 1813.

23 "Life and Letters of... Minto", II.364.

24 do., II. 365 et.seq.

25 One Philip Ferdinand de Hamilton (born in Brussels ca. 1664, who died in Vienna 1750) had been a still-life and animal painter at the Imperial Court.

26 This was Hamilton's second collection, gathered together from excavations made during 1789-90 and which was sold to England in 1798, but because of shipwreck only part of the collection arrived.

27 Count Deym was well liked at the Court of Naples and he obtained special permission to take casts from the antiques of the Museo Borbonico. (Julius Schlosser, *Geschichte der Porträtbildnerei in Wachs, "Jahrbuch der kunsthistorischen Sammlungen des allerhöchsten Kaiserhauses",* Vienna 1911.

28 The three naval squadrons were named the Blue, the Red and the White.

29 Her very first poem was dedicated to a British victory: "Lines address'd to Victory in consequence of the success of Lord Cornwallis and his Army against Tipoo Sahib. 1793."

# CHAPTER 4
## Nelson at Naples and Palermo

Let us now turn to the history of Naples[1] where we shall meet our hero at last.

A triple wedding took place in Vienna in 1790 by which the bonds between Naples and Austria became even stronger. The Crown Prince Franz of Austria married Maria Theresa; the Grand Duke Ferdinand of Tuscany married Louise, another daughter of the Queen; and the Crown Prince Franz of Naples took as his wife the Archduchess Clementine, a 13-year-old sister of the Austrian Crown Prince. (This marriage took place by proxy and was consummated in Genoa in 1797.) On July 12th 1793 Sir William Hamilton effected a treaty of confederation between Great Britain and Ireland and Naples.

On September 11th of the same year, Horatio Nelson, who was born in 1758 and married to the widow Fanny Nisbet in 1787, sailed into the Gulf of Naples

*Naples Harbour in 1784. Engraving by Giorgio Hackert after a painting by Filippo Hackert, from a series of pictures of the ports of the Two Sicilies commissioned by the Neapolitan royalty.*

on the *Agamemnon* and wrote quite unsuspectingly to his wife of his encounter with Lady Hamilton.[2]

He was given command of that ship on January 25th 1793 and by June 6th he was on service in the Mediterranean; on July 13th the blockade of Toulon was begun, and the town was occupied on the 24th. Nelson injured his right eye at Calvi (Corsica) and on March 27th he wrote to Sir William Hamilton describing the battle of Bastia. On July 15th 1795 he was sent to Genoa with a Squadron to co-operate with the Austrians. After the battle of Cape St. Vincent 14th February 1797 he was promoted Rear-Admiral of the Blue and made a Knight of the Bath. Near Santa Cruz[3] he lost his right arm (24th July 1797.)

On March 29th 1798, Nelson who at that time sailed in the well tried *Irresistible* transferred his flag to the *Vanguard*, and on June 17th, in his search for the French fleet, once again called at Naples. Lady Hamilton, already anxious for his well being, persuaded Maria Carolina to send provisions and stores to Sicily for his squadron. On July 18th he was in Alexandria and on August 1st the battle of Aboukir was joined which brought Nelson immortal fame and the French fleet irretrievable disaster. A wound on the forehead served as an outward reminder of this battle to the already war battered hero and the

*Horatio Viscount Nelson, Duke of Bronte, painted by John Hoppner, to whom we also owe one of the best portraits of Joseph Haydn. Nelson sat for the painter in 1802 in his London studio. The Battle of Copenhagen is represented in the background. An engraving published after Nelson's death changed this to the Battle of Trafalgar, in which the English national hero was killed.*

resultant headaches were a cause for solicitude to Lady Hamilton. News of this great victory did not reach the Royal Court at Naples until September 3rd. In a letter dated September 8th, Sir William already calls the victor "our bosom friend".

On September 22nd Nelson himself came to Naples, and the kingdom had by then formed a military alliance with Austria against France. He was received with storms of rejoicing and scenes of great enthusiasm, and was acclaimed a hero and liberator. The impression he made on Lady Hamilton was profound, and as she got to know him more intimately, her veneration, it seems, quickly changed to love. After a ball at Count Franz Esterházy's, the Austrian Ambassador, the Hamiltons gave a great reception on the 29th, Nelson's birthday. As early as October 4th Nelson, perhaps sensing domestic complications or fearing a surfeit of hero worship, writes to his superior in the Mediterranean, Lord St. Vincent[4] : "Naples is a dangerous place and we must keep clear of it." Already Miss Knight was writing poems eulogising Nelson while Lady Hamilton sang songs with topical words to well known tunes about his exploits[5].

,Continuing this rather dry chronological survey: At the end of October Nelson made a vain attempt to seize Malta from the French; on November 6th he was created "Baron of the Nile and Burnham Thorpe" (his birthplace in Norfolk); on December 21st the Royal Family fled to Palermo for safety; Nelson and the Hamiltons followed them two days later; there too the victor of the Nile was given a great reception, on the last day of that eventful year he made a written request to Lord St. Vincent, asking permission to retire, complaining that he considered it an insult that he should have to serve under an officer younger than himself (Sir William Sidney Smith)[6]. In the beginning of March 1799 he considered for the first time returning with the Hamiltons to England on board the *Vanguard*.

In those days Lady Hamilton repeatedly wrote to Nelson's wife in London, using the Motto of the Order of the Bath, *Tria Juncta in Uno*, in referring to Lady Nelson, the Queen of Naples and herself.[7] However, within the trio one could very well substitute Sir William for Lady Nelson, in fact the motto was interpreted in several other ways[8]. Lady Hamilton, who even before Aboukir had acted as an amateur diplomat in the service of England, was now not only the confidante of the politically alert Queen of Naples but had taken upon herself the task of unofficial secretary to Nelson himself. On March 31st 1799 Miss Knight wrote an Ode which is preserved in manuscript among the Nelson Papers in the British Museum: "Lines written after a walk at Villa Lucchesi near Palermo with Lady Hamilton and Lord Nelson."[9].

On April 5th Nelson was promoted Rear-Admiral of the Red and on June 8th he took command of the *Foudroyant*. He went to Naples on June 24th to subdue the revolutionaries, where the rebellious Admiral, Prince Francesco Caracciolo, was executed five days later in the presence of Lady Hamilton. In the middle of July Nelson refused to obey the orders of Rear-Admiral Lord Keith,[10] to take the Fleet to Minorca. Even so, ten days later, he was appointed provisional Commander-in-Chief in the Mediterranean; on August 1st Aboukir Day was celebrated in Naples and on the 8th Nelson returned to Palermo, again receiving a great ovation. On the 13th Ferdinand IV created him "Duke of Bronte" (Sicily) and Lady Hamilton received, on Nelson's instigation, the Cross of the Order of St. John from Czar Paul, the new Grand Master of the Maltese

*Lord Nelson's letter to Lady Hamilton dated 25 January 1799, with the phrases 'Nelson never changes, Nelson never abandons his friends in distress .. Nelson never quits Palermo but by the desire of the Queen'.*

Order.

Between October 5th and 22nd Nelson, despite his original refusal, took the fleet to Port Mahon in Minorca, but he was back in Palermo on the 26th. Nelson's friend, Admiral Samuel Granston Goodall, wrote to the former from London on November 15th[11]: " They say here you are Rinaldo in the arms of Armida, and that it requires the firmness of an Ubaldo, and his brother Knight, to draw you from the Enchantress".[12]   At this time Lord Arthur Paget was commissioned to go to Palermo to examine the situation there.  On the strength of his first report, which he sent from Vienna, he was marked by the Government as the successor of Sir William Hamilton.[13]   The change in the

Command in the Mediterranean had taken place even before then. Nelson's friend, Lord St. Vincent, now in very poor health, was succeeded by Keith, who was not favourably disposed towards Nelson. On January 6th 1800 Keith returned from the Atlantic and resumed the Supreme Command in the Mediterranean. General Suvorov wrote to Nelson on January 12th from Prague: *Je vous croyais de Malte en Egypte pour y écraser le reste des surnaturels athées de notre temps par les Arabes! Palermo n'est pas Cithère.*[14]

( "I thought you were going from Malta to Egypt to destroy there by the aid of the Arabs the remaining but supernatural Atheists of our time. Palermo is not Cythère.")

On January 20th Nelson, who was gradually falling into disgrace, met Keith in Leghorn (Livorno); on February 3rd they both landed in Palermo and on the 12th they were before Malta. There Keith remained while Nelson returned to Palermo on March 16th. Meanwhile, on February 18th, Nelson had captured the French ship *Le Généreux,* and on March 30th *Le Guillaume Tell,* the second of the two that had managed to elude him at Aboukir, fell into his hands. Miss Knight's "Additional Verses to God Save the King" are connected with this episode [15]. They were printed in a leaflet containing three stanzas written by her: "For the Battle of the Nile", "For the Généreux" and "For the William Tell", the last bearing the initials "E.C.K."; in addition there are two stanzas without titles, signed "Sir E.B."[16] That the first stanza was written at an earlier date we can see from a letter which Nelson had sent to his wife on September 28th 1798;[17] "Songs and sonnetti are numerous beyond what I ever could deserve. I send the additional verse to *God Save the King,* as I know you will sing it with pleasure.[18] I cannot move on foot or in a carriage, for the kindness of the populace; but good Lady Hamilton preserves all the papers as the highest treat for you."[19].

On April 22nd Paget, who had recently arrived in Naples, was installed as the new Ambassador and Sir William took his official leave. The next day he

*A medallion commemorating the coronation of Leopold II, or rather the related visit by the royal Neapolitan couple.*

and his wife accompanied Nelson on the *Foudroyant* to Malta via Syracuse, as it was expected that La Valetta, the capital, would soon be handed over (this however did not take place until September 5th). It is certain that on this journey Nelson and Emma became lovers as the birth of their daughter Horatia was to reveal (January 29th 1801).

About the time of their departure from Naples Miss Knight wrote a new poem: "Song addressed to Lady Hamilton on her birthday, April 26th 1800 on board the *Foudroyant*, in a Gale of Wind".[20]

The King's Saint's day, May 30th, was celebrated by an amnesty in Palermo. The Queen decided now to go to Vienna on a visit, with her four youngest children, to her daughter Maria Theresa; Nelson[21] who had returned with the Hamiltons on June 1st, was to take her by sea to Livorno. (He had been recalled, as it was hoped that he might now render greater services in the Northern Seas than in the Mediterranean). This visit to her daughter was undertaken by Maria Carolina with the intention of pleading in Vienna with the Austrian Government, and the Governments friendly to Austria, for resistance to Napoleon. On August 30th 1799 she had already made clear her desire to be invited to Vienna, and on April 17th 1800 she expressed her pleasure at having had her wish fulfilled[22]. Thugut[23], the foreign minister, who was just then about to conclude a permanent peace pact with France, wrote to his colleague Joseph Maria Count Colloredo[24] on May 17th that he was convinced this visit could do more harm to the affairs of His Majesty than would a lost battle. He knew Maria Carolina from his years of service in Naples and he threatened to resign within a fortnight if the Queen were to occupy herself with politics during her stay in Vienna. She consented to refrain from doing so; Thugut, however, left the Chancellery for good in October. In this connection an episode, which the author of the life of Lord Minto relates, is worth noting: "Austria by no means shared in the English sympathies for the Bourbon dynasty. When in the spring of 1800 the Duc de Berri visited Vienna, he was very coldly received by the Austrian Government.... Lord Minto, however, felt it his duty to show the Duke all possible respect, and for some weeks he resided under the roof of the English Legation"[25]. The Duke arrived in Palermo shortly before Maria Carolina's departure. She had intended to give him one of her daughters in marriage; but no wedding took place. The Queen, her daughters, and the Duke left Palermo at the same time, possibly on Nelson's ship.[26] The Duke, at a later date, made a morganatic marriage with Anna Brown in England[27] before he eventually married Princess Caroline of Naples, a grandchild of the Queen (the eldest daughter of Crown Prince Franz of Naples).

At this point we must add several excerpts from letters. In March 1800 Lord Minto, at that time English Ambassador in Vienna, wrote to his wife, who had not yet joined him[28] : "I have letters from Nelson and Lady Hamilton. It does not seem clear that he will go home. I hope he will not for his own sake, and he will at least, I hope, take Malta first. He does not seem at all conscious

*Ferdinand IV, King of the Two Sicilies, engraving by J Pichler after a painting by Kreuzinger.*
*Copies were distributed via the Artaria company*

of the sort of discredit he has fallen into, or the cause of it, for he writes still, not wisely, about Lady H. and all that. But it is hard to condemn and use ill a hero, as he is in his own element, for being foolish about a woman who has art enough to make fools of many wiser than an Admiral."

On April 6th Nelson wrote to Minto[29] : "I go with our dear friends Sir William and Lady Hamilton, but whether by water or land depends on the will of Lord Keith." On May 9th the Admiralty informed Lord Keith[30] that if Nelson's state of health made it impossible for him to carry out his duties, he would be free to come home; either by sea, if there were a possibility, or by land, if he should so prefer.[31] At first Nelson decided on the sea journey, in the hope of being able to sail in his flagship, the *Foudroyant*, all the way to England.

News from the theatre of war delayed the Queen's journey. She sailed eventually on June 10th with the two ships, *Foudroyant* and *Alexander*, which were accompanied by four Russian ships and one English frigate. The King, who had had a quarrel with the Queen just before she left, did not come to the port to see her off.  Leaving Sicily and Naples must have been as sad for Lady Hamilton as for her husband, although both were taking with them what they held dearest.  Miss Knight grasped the same opportunity for returning to her homeland, and of course Mrs. Cadogan accompanied her daughter; we shall hear later about other members of the retinue.  On June 14th, the day of Marengo, the ships entered the port of Livorno, where Maria Carolina gave her three friends farewell presents, for it was not decided until later that Nelson and the Hamiltons should travel via Vienna.  This was not only the Queen's wish, but Lady Hamilton also preferred the land route.  Miss Knight wrote to Captain Sir Edward Berry[32] from Livorno on July 2nd: "The Queen wishes, if possible, to prosecute her journey.  Lady Hamilton cannot bear the thought of going by sea; and, therefore, nothing but impracticability will prevent our going to Vienna.  Lord Nelson is well, and keeps up his spirits amazingly.  Sir William appears broken, distressed, and harassed."

Lord Keith strongly disapproved of this transport of civilians on a British man-of-war and gave other orders to the *Foudroyant*.  This was another reason why Nelson decided to go to Vienna.  On June 24th he reported to Lord Keith, who had just arrived[33]: "The idea of removing the *Foudroyant* has created an alarm at the Palace, and I send you a letter from thence.  If Sir William and Lady Hamilton go home by land, it is my intention to go with them; if by water, we shall be happy in taking the best ship we can get; but we are pledged not to quit the Royal Family until they are in perfect security."  At last Keith put the *Alexander* at their disposal, which could have taken the Queen back to Naples or to Trieste.

Our party was forced to choose the land route after all because of the French advance, which just then could have been dangerous for them.  Thus the impatient homeland was kept waiting still longer for its hero's return.  Livorno itself seemed menaced by the French invasion of Upper Italy and preparations were made for its defence; with Nelson himself as a possible commander.  On July 16th Miss Knight wrote again to Sir Edward Berry[34] : "It is, at length, decided that we go by land; and I feel all the dangers and difficulties to which we shall be exposed.  Think of our embarking on board small Austrian vessels at Ancona, for Trieste, as part of the land journey ... Lord Nelson is going on an expedition he disapproves, and against his own convictions, because he has promised the Queen, and that others advise her.  I pity the Queen.  Prince Belmonte[35] directs the march; and Lady Hamilton, though she does not like him, seconds his proposals, because she hates the sea, and wishes to visit different Courts of Germany.  Sir William says he shall die by the way, and he looks so ill, that I should not be surprised if he did."

On July 9th the Queen thought it necessary to go to Messina on board the *Alexander*[36] but she returned to Livorno on the 10th.  Apparently the letter which Lady Minto wrote from Vienna to her youngest sister, Lady Malmesbury, whom we have previously mentioned, refers to this period[37] : "Mr. Wyndham[38] arrived yesterday from Florence. He left the Queen of Naples, Sir William and Lady Hamilton, and Nelson, at Leghorn. The Queen has given up all thoughts of coming here. She asked Lord Keith in her own proper person for the Foudroyant to take her back. He refused positively giving her such a ship. She has three frigates of her own lying at Leghorn, but she said she could not trust them, and he told her all he could do was to give her a frigate, for he did not know what occasion he might have for a ship of the line. She is very ill with a sort of convulsive fit, and Nelson is staying there to nurse her; he does not intend going home until he has escorted her back to Palermo. His zeal for the public service seems entirely lost in his love and vanity and they all sit and flatter each other all day long. When Lord Keith refused the *Foudroyant*, the Queen wept, concluding that royal tears were irresistible; but he remained unmoved and would grant nothing but a frigate to convoy her own frigates to Trieste. He told her Lady Hamilton had had command of the fleet long enough. She was still at Leghorn. - It is said that much of the cruelty at Naples is owing to Lady Hamilton[39] , and that if she were to appear there she would be torn to pieces".

At last, after a month of delays the Queen with her children and retinue left Livorno. She was accompanied by Nelson and the Hamiltons together with Miss Knight and Mrs. Cadogan, as well as their own attendants. On July 12th the two parties arrived in Florence; the Court of Tuscany had been absent from that city for a year and was staying in Vienna. Two days later the Queen set out for Ancona and the Adriatic via Arezzo and Foligno, as Bologna and Sarzana were already occupied by the French. Nelson and his party followed on July 16th and were received everywhere with great acclamation. Near Castell San Giovanni (South of Perugia) their carriage broke down and Sir William and Lady Hamilton received minor injuries. A similar incident occurred at Arezzo, where Mrs. Cadogan and Miss Knight were forced to stay behind until their carriage was repaired while Nelson and the Hamiltons hastened to join the Queen, with the French steadily advancing. On July 24th they were all reunited at Ancona. On the same day Miss Knight again wrote to Sir Edward Berry:[40]

"We left Leghorn the day after I wrote to you by Mr.Tyson[41], and ... arrived in twenty six hours at Florence ... after a short stay, we proceeded on our way to this place ... at length, however, we arrived at Ancona".

Here they found the Austrian frigate *Bellona*, which had taken Pope Pius VII back to the Papal States, and a Russian Squadron which was about to sail to Corfu. This squadron, consisting of the *Nawarskij* and two frigates as well as a brigantine, was under the command of the Dalmatian Count Vojnovic. As it appeared too dangerous to use the Austrian frigate *Bellona*, the Queen and Nelson sailed in a ship belonging to the Russian squadron; the *Bellona* however accompanied them. In place of the Commandant of the brigantine, who had fallen ill, First Lieutenant Capaci, an inept and arrogant Neapolitan who aroused

*Maria Carolina, Queen of the Two Sicilies, in 1777. Engraving by Raphael Morghen. The daughter of Maria Theresa is represented here at the age of 20.*

Nelson's anger, led the squadron. Miss Knight and Mrs. Cadogan sailed in one of the three frigates under the command of an old Englishman named Messer. The Queen and Sir William were violently sea-sick and so were many of the attendants. This is how the party arrived in Trieste on August 1st 1800.

1 Cf. Alexander Freiherr von Helfert's two books, *Königin Caroline von Neapel und Sicilien im Kampfe gegen die französische Weltherrschaft 1790-1814*, Vienna 1878; and *Maria Karolina von Österreich ... Anklagen und Verteidigung*, Vienna 1884.

2 "A young woman of amiable manners, and who does honour to the station of which she is raised" (The Dispatches and Letters of Vice Admiral Lord Viscount Nelson, with notes by Sir Nicholas Harris Nicolas, G.C.M.G.", London 1845, I. 326).

3 The capital of Teneriffe, the largest of the Canary Isles.

4 "The Dispatches and Letters of...Nelson", III.144 et.seq.- John Jervis, Earl of St. Vincent, was Commander in the Mediterranean until June 15th 1799.

5 Sichel's "Emma Lady Hamilton", pp.226, 231, 372 and 495.

6 The chief cause for Nelson's later discontent was that he had been prevented from cutting Napoleon's retreat from Egypt.

7 Lady Hamilton wrote to Nelson on October 4th 1798 from Caserta: "I told her Majesty [Maria Carolina] we only wanted Lady Nelson to be the female *tria juncta in uno*, for we all love you, and yet all three differently, and yet all equally - if you can make that out." (Walter Sichel, "Emma Lady Hamilton" p.496).

8 On October 24th 1799 Nelson wrote to Lord Minto: "... Sir William Hamilton, Lady Hamilton, and myself, we are the real *Tria juncta in uno*". ("The Dispatches and Letters of ...Nelson" IV. 63.)

9 Nelson Papers (British Museum), et.seq. 113 et.seq., 2 pp. Quarto, signed "E:C:K:".

10 The new Commander in the Mediterranean.

11 "The Dispatches and Letters of ...Nelson", IV.205.

12 Cf. Tasso, *La Gerusalemime Liberata*.

13 Hamilton was recalled on January 16th 1800.

14 "The Athenaeum", 1876, I.396.

15 "Nelson Papers", et.seq. 149-150, 4 pp.Octavo.

16 Sir Edward Berry was Flag Captain to Nelson at the Battle of the Nile and in Command of the *Foudroyant* when it seized the *Généreux* and the *Guillaume Tell*. Miss Knight's three stanzas are preserved in manuscript in the "Nelson Papers" (et. seq. 148, 2 pp. fol.), together with the original stanzas and a sixth stanza, possibly also by Miss Knight. Cf. her autobiography, I. 122.

17 Thomas Joseph Pettigrew, "Memoirs of the Life of Vice Admiral Lord Viscount Nelson, K.B., Duke of Bronte, etc. etc.", London 1849, I. 153.

18 This, Sir N.H. Nicolas (the editor of Nelson's letters) said, has been attributed to a Mr. Devonport. It was written by Miss Knight.

19 On September 8th (et. seq.) 1798 Lady Hamilton had written to Nelson from Naples (Sichel's "Emma Lady Hamilton", p.488): "I send you some Sonets, but I must have taken a ship on purpose to send you all written on you."

20 Printed on pp3 and 4 of the already mentioned "Additional Verses" (Nelson Papers, fol. 151). The song went "to the old tune of 'Hearts of Oak'", says Miss Knight in her autobiography, pp.146 et. seq. In the 89th volume of the "Nelson Papers" there is on f.158 (2 pp. quarto) another handwritten poem by Miss Knight, without title, which begins: "Come fair Erato, Muse of Love"; followed by further poems of hers to Maria Carolina, Ferdinand IV and Lady Hamilton, all of them written at Naples.

21 On June 2nd, Nelson was awarded the Grand Cross of the Order of St Ferdinand and Merit, created by Ferdinand IV on April 1st 1800.

22 Alexander Freiherr von Helfert, *Memorie segrete. Des Freiherrn Giangiacomo von Cresceri Enthüllungen über den Hof von Neapel 1796 - 1816*, Vienna, 1892, pp.48 et. seq.

23 Nelson did not have a high opinion of him (see his letter to Lord Minto from Palermo, August 20th 1799. "The Dispatches and Letters of...Nelson", III.452)

24 Alfred von Vivenot, *Vertrauliche Briefe des Freiherrn v. Thugut*, Vienna 1872, II. 218.

25 "Life and Letters of...Minto", III.75,note.

26Cf. *Die Erinnerungen des Grafen Roger von Damas.* Paris 1912, I. 316; English selection: London 1913, p.284.

27 In about 1808, he saw Lady Hamilton's "Attitudes" in London ("Memoirs of Madame Vigée-Lebrun", translated by L. Strachey, London 1904, p.69).

28 "Life and Letters of...Minto", III. 114.

29 "The Dispatches and Letters of...Nelson", IV.222.

30 do., IV.242.

31 Lord Spencer, Chief of the Admiralty, wrote a friendly letter to Nelson on the same day, but reproached him for having been "in an inactive situation at a Foreign Court."

32 "The Dispatches and Letters of...Nelson", IV.263.

33 "The Dispatches and Letters of...Nelson", IV.260 et. seq.

34 "The Dispatches and Letters of ... Nelson, IV.263 et.seq.

35 Marchese Galatona Pignatelli, Prince de Belmonte, was believed to be the Queen's lover.

36 Nelson had hoisted his flag on board the *Alexander* on June 28th.

37 "Life and Letters of ... Minto", III.139 et. seq.

38 British Minister to Tuscany.

39 This assumption is disputed.

40 "The Dispatches and Letters of ... Nelson IV.264

41 Captain John Tyson acted as Nelson's secretary.

*Bernardo Bellotto, called Canaletto, painted this very famous view of Vienna, seen from the Belvedere, around 1760*

# CHAPTER 5
## *Vienna about 1800*

To give an idea of the atmosphere prevailing in Vienna at the time when it was threatened by Napoleon, let us first acquaint ourselves with two English people, a man and a woman, of whom we shall hear more in later chapters.

Sir Gilbert Elliot, First Earl of Minto (1751-1814), Governor General of India from 1807-1814, was Envoy Extraordinary and Minister Plenipotentiary at the Court of Vienna from 1799 till 1801[1]. His official appointment did not take place before June 20th 1800, when he brought about the alliance between Austria and England; and he was recalled when this alliance was broken up by the Peace of Lunéville, on February 9th 1801. In 1777 he married Anna Maria, the eldest daughter of Sir George Amyand, by whom he had six children, three sons and three daughters. His biography from which we have already quoted

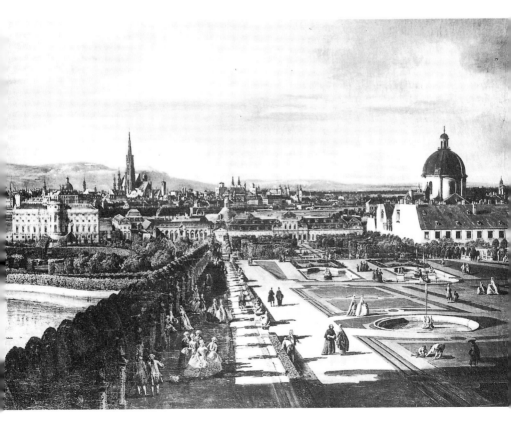

*The Kohlmarkt in Vienna. On the*
*night is the Michaelerkirche,*
*adjacent to the so-called*
*Michaelerhaus. where Haydn lived*
*in the 1750s. Engraving by Carl*
*Schutz, 1786.*

("Life and Letters of Sir Gilbert Elliot, First Earl of Minto", London 1874) also contains letters to his wife who later joined him in Vienna. In them Lord Minto describes his first impressions of that city, which we shall quote as far as they have a bearing on later events. In August 1799 Lord Minto writes (III.71 et. seq.): "Madame de Thun, who has been so long the centre of the society of Europe, and is a plain, agreeable, sensible woman, with three agreeable daughters, all married, is unfortunately very ill and her family is alarmed for her... The three daughters of Madame de Thun are most pleasing women, in the best style of English gentlewomen ... All this family talk English, or at least understand it perfectly." The beautiful and intelligent Countess Wilhelmine Thun, née Comtesse Ulfeld, who with Gluck, Mozart, Haydn and Beethoven had played a very special role in the musical history of Vienna, died a few months after this letter was written, on May 8th 1800. One of her three lovely

daughters - the "Three Graces" as the Anglo-German globe-trotter George Forster called them - Elisabeth, was married to Count (later Prince) Rasumofsky, the Russian Ambassador in Vienna and friend of Maria Carolina[2]; the second, Marie Christine, was the wife of Prince Karl Lichnowsky, also of Vienna (both played important parts in the lives of Mozart and Beethoven); the youngest, Maria Carolina, (1769-1800), married the English Attaché to the Legation in Vienna in 1793, Richard Meade afterwards the second Earl of Clanwilliam[3] . Among others who wrote about the mother of these three ladies were Swinburne, Wraxall, Moore and Burney; the latter met her in the house of the English Ambassador Lord Stormont (David Murray, Viscount Stormont) in 1772[4] .

In September 1799 Lord Minto writes[5] : "I have assisted lately at a most noble chasse at the Prince Nicholas Esterházy's three posts from Vienna[6] . We were eighteen sportsmen and 1,000 attendants.  I was myself attended by three peasants carrying on their backs each a stand with seven guns, and I had three servants to load for me.  We killed in the forenoon upwards of a thousand pieces of game, and strange to say I shot like Robin Hood, and killed 120 pieces of game, viz. pheasants, hares, partridges, myself.  We dined with a beautiful princess and returned to Vienna.  It is really a royal style, and a thing to do once...What you will enjoy here is the love of country life, at least in summer."[7] Prince Nikolaus II (1765-1833), the fourth Esterházy to have Haydn in his service, had been ruling since 1794.  He moved occasionally from one to another of his various castles but resided mostly in Eisenstadt, where musical life enjoyed a marked revival at that time.  His wife was Marie Hermenegilde, née Princess Liechtenstein[8] (1769-1845), to whom Beethoven later dedicated his Opus 45 - three marches for Piano Duo.  Prince Esterházy, apart from being a great lover of music, was a distinguished collector of works of art; the picture gallery, housed in his summer palace (formerly owned by Kaunitz) in the suburb of Mariahilf,  was later given to the Hungarian National Gallery in Budapest.

Before considering any further Lord Minto's impressions of Vienna and its surroundings, we must now - for the sake of chronological sequence - turn our attention to the lady to whom we referred at the beginning of this chapter. Melesina St. George, née Chenevix, a young widow from Ireland, who later married Mr. Richard Trench, came to the Imperial City on a pleasure trip in the Spring of 1800; her "Journal kept during a visit to Germany in 1799, 1800" was published in London in 1861 by her son, R.C.Trench, then Dean of Westminster, later Archbishop of Dublin.  He issued this privately printed book in 1862 in enlarged form, under the title "Remains", and it is from this later version that we shall quote.  The journey took the lady in 1800 from Dresden via Prague to Vienna (26th March to 18th July) including an excursion to Baden, the nearby Spa, then via Prague, Carlsbad and Teplitz back to Dresden (August 27th et. seq.) where we shall meet her again.  Mrs. St. George writes in her Journal on April 13th 1800, (p.68): "At Prince Schwarzenberg's[9] I heard Haydn's famous 'Creation', a very pleasing oratorio but which I think is applauded here much above its merit... I have met likewise with a very amiable woman to whom the Countess Münster recommended me.  She is a Berlinoise, and the widow of Prince Reuss, but is received in very few of the first circles here, on account of her birth, her father having been a merchant.  She was originally a Jewess.  I went to Mr. Arnstein's with her, which I fear was a breach of etiquette.  Madm. Arnstein being a banker's wife, and of the second class of noblesse.  However, I found there a pleasant society, and an easier tone than in most houses at Vienna.  She keeps open house every evening to a few women, and all the best company in Vienna as to men.  She is a pretty woman with an excellent address."  We shall hear more about the Arnstein family later on.

On April 17th 1800 Mrs. St.George further writes, (p.70): "I dined to-day at Prince Esterházy's, one of the greatest among the Hungarian noblemen.  He has

*One of Ferdinand Bergl's frescoes in the Archbishop's Palace in Ober-St.Veit. They date from 1760 and still adorn the Garden Room today.*

a million florin[10] a year, but is greatly in debt. He was not at home, but the Princess is a charming, unaffected pretty woman about thirty." This was in the Vienna Town Palace, in the *Wallner-Strasse*.

On June 6th we read in her journal (pp. 79 et. seq.): "I passed this morning with Mad. de la Gardie, wife to the Swedish Minister[11] .... We went together to see Füger's paintings. He is a fine artist and sincere enthusiast. I believe he ranks very high in the first class of historical painters ... I also saw his drawings from Klopstock's Messiah - wild, fanciful expressive... Füger is a tall, well-looking man, about forty, his countenance is placid, his eye is open, clear, and attractive - I mean, invites you to look into it, and to repose your soul in his. I have seen this in but few eyes and they generally belong to persons who combined genius with simplicity ... In the evening went to Lady Minto's and Madm. Arnstein's"... Füger too we shall meet in connection with Nelson.

On June 11th she writes (p.81): "The Emperor has done everything within the bounds of decent respect to prevent the Queen of Naples from coming; but cannot succeed." And lastly, on June 15th to 17th (p.82) we read: "Three days at Baden, a small town two posts from Vienna, celebrated for its warm sulphurous baths." This place too, will be of interest to us.

And now again for order's sake, we must return to Lord Minto. On May 2nd his wife had arrived in Vienna, and six weeks later he describes[12] his family's new home to Lady Palmerston:[13] "St. Veit: June 17th 1800 I should wish to give you a notion of our present life and conversation. We are from Vienna, the distance Roehampton is from London. Our House stands on the side of a hill rising above a plain dotted with villages and villas, and watered by the Wien[14] . From the river the view is beautiful. Mountains covered with wood, valleys and dells, and a magnificent park of the Emperor's[15]. The hill above us rises into vineyards, and is crowned by the Emperor's park. Our house was once a monastery, and is now the Bishop of Vienna's palace; it is extremely spacious, the garden in the old style; straight walks and parterres, with temples and water-spouts and cascades; but there is gravel, and grass and shade... There is good fishing, and we have open carriages of various fashions and capacities. One of them carries eight of us. The drives, rides and walks are beautiful beyond description." The old castle of *Ober-Sankt-Veit*, which is still standing next to the church, dominates the suburb of the same name, which now forms part of district 13 of Vienna. It had been the summer residence of the Archbishops of Vienna for a long time, and it was owned by the Emperor only from 1762 until 1765. The new parts were added in 1660 and its present form dates from 1742, though it was restored in 1817. It is a two storey building with a square inner court; only parts of the park remain. The frescoes by Johann Bergl (about 1760) in the garden-rooms, which were badly restored in 1894, depict, among other subjects, river scenes, such as a sailing ship at anchor, natives carrying their wares and ship's crews receiving and examining them. This castle, about which we shall have more to say, was rented by the English Ambassador about 1800 and occupied, it seems, for the whole year.

Again Mrs. St. George notes on June 27th, (pp. 84,et. seq.): "In the evening went to see a fireworks display in the Prater. The emplacement is perfectly convenient, the view beautiful, and the representation extremely amusing. Those spectators who chose to pay a florin are seated on a stage, exactly opposite where there is no crowd, and where they are perfectly at their ease. The difference of colour in the fire, some being perfectly white, some bright yellow, has a good effect, and there is a degree of perspective obtained, beyond what I thought possible. The performance represented the taking of Genoa.[16] .". At that time Lady Minto, who was possibly present at the same performance, wrote to her sister Lady Malmesbury[17] about this popular form of entertainment in Vienna in the *Prater* on the island which constitutes the suburb Leopoldstadt, between the Danube and the so-called *Donaukanal* (nearer the City): "It was splendid, and the evening such as you never see in England; and I assure you I

have seen nothing here that does not surpass my expectations."
Under the dates of July 3rd to 7th Mrs. St. George mentions the Arnstein family once more (p.86): "I dined also again with the Arnsteins, who I see hate the Austrian government. She is a Prussian, and according to the late cant phrase, 'that accounts for it'." And on July 14th, shortly before her departure, she writes (P.88): "Was presented at Duke Albert's [of Sachsen-Teschen], where I thought myself in England ... He is son to the late King of Poland".[18] Another personage we shall meet again in connection with Nelson.

1 As successor to Sir Morton Eden.
2 From 1779 until 1781 he had been Attaché at the Russian Legation in Naples. His wife was in Naples in 1806; cf. the "Memoires" of Roger, Count de Damas, Inspector General of the Neapolitan Army (edited by J. Rambaud, Paris 1912).
3 As "Lady Guildford de Gilhall" she appeared in 1795 among the subscribers to Beethoven's Op.1, the three great Piano Trios.
4 Burney, "The Present State of Music in Germany etc", 2nd major ed., London 1775. I. 258 et. seq. and 295 et. seq., 393, etc.
5 "Life and Letters of ...Minto", III.73 et. seq.
6 Minto apparently visited the Esterházys at Eisenstadt. Michael Kelly ("Reminiscences", London 1826, I.218 et. seq.), although he mentions this place, seems to have stayed at Esterház, the other castle of the noble family.
7 Cf. Richard Bright, "Travels from Vienna through Lower Hungary", Edinburgh 1818,p.346 et. seq.
8 Marie Louise Elisabeth Vigée-Le Brun, who had come from Rome in 1792 with her newly painted portrait of Lady Hamilton (as Sibylla), also painted the portraits of Princess Esterházy and of the Countess Rasumofsky.
9 Joseph Johann Prince Schwarzenberg, in whose Vienna Town Palace on the *Neuer Markt* the first performance of Haydn's "Creation" had taken place on April 29th 1798. Mrs. St. George is referring to a later performance.
10 1 florin, the Austrian Gulden.
11 Jakob Gustav de la Gardie had been married exactly one year to Kristina Amalia Hedwig Adelaide Sparre af Söfdeborg.
12 "Life and Letters of... Minto", III.117.
13 Mary, daughter of Benjamin Thomas Mee, married in 1783 to Henry Temple, second Viscount Palmerston (she was his second wife): the parents of the great statesman.
14 The Wien is a tributary of the Danube coming from the West and flowing into it opposite the Prater.
15 The *Kaiserlicher Tiergarten*, a huge hunting territory, part of the Vienna Woods, today *Lainzer Tiergarten*.
16 The capture of Genoa: April 19th until June 5th 1800, by the Austrians.
17 "Life and Letters of ... Minto", III.123.
18 August III.

# CHAPTER 6
## *Nelson's Popularity in Vienna*

In Vienna Nelson became extremely popular after his victory of Aboukir. This was not only due to the personal ties between the Courts of Austria and Naples; neither can the enmity between Austria and France wholly account for it. Nelson was the first commander to defeat Buonaparte and for that reason alone he was regarded as an almost mythical hero. But in the eyes of the Austrians, and of the Viennese in particular, he was first and foremost a romantic figure, reminiscent in some respects of Prince Eugene of Savoy.[1]

Nelson's popularity was evident in Vienna even before the end of 1798, when Lady Hamilton was practically unknown in the city[2] and when nobody could foretell that the romantic pair would ever visit Vienna. It is perhaps no coincidence, but rather a characteristic of Vienna and - as we shall see - of the countries under the Habsburgs in general, that such signs of popularity should first appear in the realms of art and fashion.

On September 22nd, 1798, barely two months after the Battle of the Nile, the outcome of which could only recently have been learned[3] , the official *Wiener Zeitung,* which usually carried advertisements of the book, art and music trades, printed the following announcement of Artaria & Co. (Supplement to No.76,p.2879) :

> *Das Porträt des Admirals Sir H. Nelson. Nach einem Original-gemälde des berühmten Orme in pathologischer* [sic!] *Manier punsiert von J.Neidl. - Man glaubt, dass bei gegenwärtigen Ereignissen dem Publikum dieses besonders schöne und vollkommen ähnliche Porträt eines so grossen Mannes angenehm sein wird, dessen ausgezeichnete Heldentaten in der Geschichte Englands Epoche machen. Ein sehr reiner Abdruck kostet 1 fl.*

("The portrait of Admiral Sir H. Nelson. Stippled in pathological [sic!] manner by J.Neidl, after an original painting by the famous Orme. - It is believed that in view of present events the public will be pleased with this particularly beautiful portrait giving a complete likeness of such a great man, whose extraordinary acts of heroism mark an epoch in the history of England. A very clear impression costs 1 fl.")

This portrait was engraved by Johann Joseph Neidl, of Vienna, after a miniature by Daniel Orme, who in 1799 exhibited a portrait of Lady Nelson in London. About 1795 Neidl engraved for Artaria the beautiful gouache-painting of Haydn by Johann Zitterer (at the piano, with the score of the Andante from the "Surprise Symphony" open before him) and a portrait of Prince Nikolaus II Esterházy. Haydn, towards the end of his life owned this Nelson print, the

*Lord Nelson, engraving by Joseph Neidl after the painting by Daniel Orme. This impression was published by the Artaria company.*

model of which is reproduced in Hilda Gamlin's "Nelson's Friendships" (London 1899, 1.265). Three months later the *Wiener Zeitung* (22nd December 1798, No. 102, p.2873) contained the following advertisement:

> *Musikalische Ankündigung. Unser Herr Wanhal, welcher sich durch eine Reihe von Jahren als musikalischer Schriftsteller in Stücken aller Art aus die uneigennützigste Weise rühmlich bekannt gemacht hat, zeichnete sich vorzüglich die letzte Kriegszeit durch Verfassung verschiedener Gelegenheitsstücke aus, welche der Unterfertigte nach und nach unter der Adresse Joseph Eder u. Comp. im Stiche verlegte. Unter diesen Musikstücken hatten 3 charakteristische Klaviersonaten das besondere Glück, allen Ständen*

*am meisten zu gefallen: denn seine "Schlacht bei Würzburg" wurde*
*selbst in Feindes Landen gesuchet und an die höchsten Höfe Europas*
*gesendet: die ah.k.k. Familie schenkte ihr das allergnädigste*
*Wohlgefallen. - Ein so ungeteilter Beifall konnte nicht anders als für*
*den Herrn Verfasser schmeichelhaft sein und ihn zur Fortsetzung*
*ähnlicher Arbeiten aufmuntern. - Er hat also seine wenigen übrigen*
*Stunden dahin verwendet, über die letzte merkwürdige Zeitgeschichte*
*eine vierte charakteristische Sonate zu schreiben. Betitelt: Die grosse*
*See-Schlacht bei Abukir, gesetzt fürs Piano-Forte, welche aus des*
*Unterzeichneten Verlag für 1 fl.20 kr. täglich zu haben ist: In Wien bei*
*Herrn Kunst- und Musikalienhändler Träg in der Singerstrasse, oder*
*in des Herrn Verfassers Wohnung in der Kärntnerstrasse beim*
*Greifen, die hintere Stiege im Hofe links, im 2ten Stock links die letzte*
*Tür. Auswärts in jeder der vorzüglichsten Handlungen der*
*Provinzialhauptstädte, oder durch postfreie Briefe an den*
*Unterzeichneten. - Das ganz abgenutzte Werk obiger "Schlacht bei*
*Würzburg" wird wieder ganz neu gestochen, und da es in einer Arbeit*
*gehet, mit einem neuen militärischen Rondo versehen, nächstens*
*erscheinen. - Ignaz Sauer, Inhaber des Kunstverlages der 7*
*Schwestern in Wien, in der Währingergasse im k.k. Waisenhaus*
*wohnhaft.*

("Musical announcement. Our Mr Wanhal[4] who in the course of a number of years has won for himself in the most disinterested way great appreciation as a writer of music of all kinds, distinguished himself particularly during the last war by works written to mark special occasions, which the undersigned engraved and published from the address of Joseph Eder & Co. Among these musical works three characteristic Piano Sonatas had the special good fortune of pleasing all classes; his "Battle of Würzburg"[5] was sought even in enemy countries and sent to the most exalted Courts of Europe; the most exalted Imperial Royal family received it with most gracious appreciation. - This general success could not but flatter the author and encourage him to continue writing similar works. He employed his rare leisure hours to write a fourth characteristic Sonata on the latest memorable events of our time, with the title: "The great Sea-Battle of Aboukir', arranged for the Piano-Forte, which can be obtained any day at the publishing house of the undersigned for 1 fl. 20 kr.: in Vienna from Mr. Träg, art and music dealer, in the Singerstrasse, or from the author's flat in the Kärntnerstrasse *beim Greifen*, the back-staircase on the left of the courtyard, second floor, last door on the left. Outside Vienna, in all the best shops of the Provincial capitals, or post-free from the undersigned. The above "Battle of Würzburg"[6] the plates of which are completely worn by use, is being newly engraved and will shortly appear - since it entails only one process - supplied with a new military Rondo. Ignaz Sauer, proprietor of the *Kunstverlag der 7 Schwestern* (The Seven Sisters Arts Publishing House) in

Vienna, in the Währingergasse, in the kk.*Waisenhaus.*)

    The only copy of this work, one of the first battle pieces[7] before Beethoven's unfortunate "Battle of Vittoria" (Wellington's victory in Spain) is preserved at the *Gesellschaft der Musikfreunde* in Vienna. Its title reads:

> *Die grosse Seeschlacht bei Abukir vom 1ten bis 3ten August 1798/ eine charakteristische Sonate/fürs/Clavier oder Piano-Forte/von/Herrn Johann Wanhal/aus Verehrung zugeeignet/dem Helden/Sir Horatio Nelson/Baron vom Nil und von Burnham Thorpe,/Contre Admiral der englischen Marine,/Wien im Kunstverlag der sieben Schwestern. 1 f 20Kr.*

("The great sea-battle of Aboukir from the 1st to the 3rd of August 1798/ a characteristic Sonata/for/the Clavichord or the Piano-Forte/by/Mr Johann Wanhal/ dedicated with respect/to the Hero/Sir Horatio Nelson/Baron of the Nile and of Burnham Thorpe/Rear-Admiral of the English Navy/Vienna, in the Seven Sisters Arts Publishing house. 1 f 20kr.")

The laurel wreath adorning the title is printed in green, and the ornamental bow in blue and white. The work contains 11 printed pages in oblong folio and bears the publisher's plate mark "S.S.24". The publishing firm was still in its infancy, but its owner, to whom at the second occupation of Vienna by the French were entrusted valuable books from the *Hofbibliothek* to hide from the enemy, seems to have been blessed with seven daughters, who provided him with the name for his publishing business.

Accompanying the movements of this "characteristic Sonata", which in itself is typically insignificant, we find the following explanatory notes describing the music:

> *Introduction. Die hohe Admiralität in London ernennt den Sir Horatio Nelson zum Befehlshaber der Flotte. Maestoso. Die englische Mannschaft begibt sich an Bord. - Allegro moderato. Admiral Nelson erteilt Befehl zur Abfahrt. Die Anker werden gelichtet. Spannung der Segel. Die Schiffe segeln ab. Die feindlich französische Flotte wird im mittelländischen Meere gesichtet. Die Avisoschiffe entdecken die feindliche Flotte und bringen Nachricht. Kriegsrat hierüber - Tempo Militare. Nelson ermuntert das Schiffsvolk zur Seeschlacht. Die Mannschaft ist bereit zu siegen oder zu sterben. Signal zum Angriff. Die Flotte nähert sich der feindlichen und greift an. Der Angriff wird lebhaft. Anfang der Kanonade. Starkes Kanonenfeuer. Die Engländer durchbrechen die feindliche Linie. Sie setzen dem feindlichen Admiralschiff heftig zu. Dieses brennet und springet in die Luft. Allgemeine Betäubung und Totenstille. Fassung und erneuerter Angriff. Der Angriff wird noch lebhafter. Das heftigste Kanonenfeuer aus vollen Ladungen. Allgemeine Jagd auf die in Unordnung geratene feindliche Flotte. Die Engländer kentern.⁸ Zwei feindliche Schiffe brennen und krachen. Andere werden verfolget. Diese streichen die Flagge. Einige Schiffe suchen sich durch die Flucht zu retten. Die feindliche Flotte wird geschlagen und fast ganz vernichtet. Das gestrandete englische Schiff wird wieder flott. Siegesgeschrei bei den Engländern. - Andante. Die englische Nation empfängt den Helden. - Finale all Inglese. Siegesfeier.*

("Introduction. The High Admiralty in London appoints Sir Horatio Nelson Command of the Fleet. *Maestoso.* The English crew goes aboard. *Allegro Moderato.* Admiral Nelson gives orders for departure. The anchors are weighed. Hoisting of the sails. The ships depart. The French fleet is sighted in the Mediterranean. The dispatch boats discover the enemy fleet and bring the news. Council of war. *Tempo Militare.* Nelson exhorts the crews to give battle. The crews are ready to conquer or die. Signal for the attack. The fleet closes on the enemy and attacks. The attack becomes lively. Beginning of the cannonade. Heavy cannon fire. The English break through the enemy's line.

They furiously attack the enemy's flag ship. It is set on fire and blows up. General stupefaction and dead silence. Recovery and renewed attack. The attack becomes even livelier. The most intense cannon fire from full broadsides. General pursuit of the disordered enemy fleet. [An English ship capsizes][9] . Two enemy ships collide and burn. Others are being chased. Some strike their flags. A few ships try to save themselves by flight. The enemy Fleet is beaten and almost entirely destroyed. The stranded English ship is righted again. Victory shouts from the English. *Andante*. The English Nation welcomes the hero.[10] - *Finale all Inglese*[11] . Victory celebrations.")

That Sauer, who at the time was without a publishing licence, chose the publisher Träg as commissioner, may be explained by the fact that Eder, whom he had previously employed, had himself meanwhile become editor of a Nelson work. As early as November 14th 1798, the *Wiener Zeitung* (No. 97, p.3658) printed an advance notice announcing more than twenty numbers of a *Musikalische Monatsschrift* (Musical Monthly), which Ferdinand Kauer, another fashionable composer of Vienna, intended to publish. On December 5th 1798, Eder and the composer offered as the first number of this series:

*Nelson's grosse See-Schlacht für das Forte-Piano mit Begleitung einer Violin, und Violoncello verfasst, und zugeeignet Seiner Königlichen Hoheit August, Prinz von England. Von Ferdinand Kauer, Wien, auf dem Graben in der Joseph Ederischen Kunst- und Muskalien-Handlung, No. 116. 2f.*

("Nelson's great sea-battle for the Forte-Piano written with accompaniment of a violin and violoncello, and dedicated to His Royal Highness Augustus, Prince of England[12] by Ferdinand Kauer. Vienna, Graben in Joseph Eder's Arts and Music shop. No.116.2f.")

One copy of this work was found in the Vienna *Stadtbibliothek*, and another is in the *Preussische Staatsbibliothek* in Berlin. This publication is in three parts: the pianoforte score in 15 pages oblong folio, the strings in 5 and 4 pages folio respectively. On the bottom half of the last page of the piano score a complete description is given. The various events in this action are numbered and given in the Piano score itself; they correspond with the movements of the music as follows: *Allegro 1, Andante 2-4, Marcia 5, Allegro 6-11, più Allegro 12-17, Andantino 18-19, Allegro 20*. Here is the explanation of the music as given in the publication itself:

*No. 1 Introduction. Vorteilhafte Stellung der französischen Flotte bei Abukir in Aegypten. - No. 2. Nelsons Entschlossenheit, dieselbe anzugreifen. - No. 3. Nelsons Aufruf an das Schiffsvolk, Vorbereitung zum Tod oder zum Sieg. - No. 4. Das Lavieren der kleineren Schiffe. No. 5. Seemarsch der [sich] nähernden englischen Flotte. - No. 6. Der mutvolle Angriff. - No. 7. Durchbrechung der französischen Linie. - No. 8. Heftige Kanonade. - No. 9. Das französische Admiralschiff L'Orient gerät in Brand. - No. 10. Fliegt in die Luft. - No. 11. Allgemeine Betäubung und plötzlich unterbrochene Kanonade. -*

*First page of the piano part of the setting of the Battle of Aboukir for piano trio, by another Viennese composer of the day, Ferdinand Kauer.*

*No. 12. Das Treffen beginnt auf das Neue. - No. 13. Kanonade und Gefecht mit doppelter Wut. - No. 14. Timoleon und Artemise brennen. - No. 15. Flucht und Verfolgung des Wilhelm Tell, Généreux, der Diane und Justice. - No. 16. Die übrigen französischen Schiffe streichen ihre Flaggen. - No. 17. Das gestrandete englische Schiff Culloden wird flott. - No. 18. Uebernahme der französischen Schiffe. - No. 19. Verpflegung der Verwundeten, Aufnahme der Gefangenen, Begrabung der Toten. - No. 20. Freudenfest über den erhaltenen Sieg.*

("No. 1. Introduction. Advantageous position of the French fleet before Aboukir in Egypt. No. 2. Nelson's determination to attack the fleet. No. 3. Nelson's appeal to the crews. Preparation for death or victory. No. 4. Manoeuvring of the smaller ships. No. 5. The approach of the English fleet. No. 6. The courageous attack. No. 7. Breakthrough of the enemy's line. No. 8. Violent cannonade. No. 9. The French flag-ship *L'Orient* is set on fire. No. 10. She blows up. No. 11. General stupefaction and sudden pause in the cannonade. No. 12. The battle is resumed. No.13. Cannonade and combat with renewed fury. No. 14. *Timoléon and Artémise* are on fire. No.15. Escape and pursuit of the *Guillaume Tell, Généreux*[13], *Diane* and *Justice*. No. 16. The remaining French ships strike their flags. No. 17. The stranded English ship *Culloden* is refloated. No. 18. Surrender of the French ships. No. 19. Tending of the wounded, reception of the prisoners, burial of the dead. No. 20. Celebration of the victory.")

*A pictorial representation of the sea-battle at Aboukir was drawn by Carl Schutz in Vienna and sold as an engraving by the Artaria company.*

Following this explanation, which is here corrected according to the advance notice of the series, there follows a *Notabene: Zur zweiten Monatsschrift ist der Gegenstand:- eine grosse Sonate für das Forte piano, Violin und Violoncello aus Mozarts Zauberflöte.*

("The subject of the second monthly periodical: a great Sonata for the Forte piano, Violin and Violoncello from Mozart's 'Magic Flute'.")

It is evident that these two competitors were not at a loss to say in music what could not be said in words. Kauer's work was performed on December 23rd 1798, in the *Leopoldstädter Theater*[14] . The composer of the then famous musical play *Das Donauweibchen* (The Nymph of the Danube) held the post of conductor[15] in this the oldest of the three Viennese suburban theatres[16]. Incidentally as though to confirm once more his familiarity with the watery element, Kauer's oratorio *Die Sintflut* (The Flood) was performed in the *Leopoldstädter Theater* on December 24th 1809; for which as can be seen from the *Allgemeine Musikzeitung* of Leipzig, special scenery was devised. Both concerts were given for charity.

In the autumn of 1798, Josef von Hammer,[17] later a famous orientalist in Vienna, wrote a poem *Auf den Sieg der Britten vor Alexandria* (On the victory of the British before Alexandria) which appeared in the December number of Wieland's periodical: *Der Neue Teutsche Merkur*[18] ; this poem is contained in the Appendix of this book.

*Engravings of Nelson's victory at Aboukir were also sold in London. One of these engravings, or one by Schütz, was found in Haydn's collection.*

Three months after the publication of the two musical battle pictures in honour of Nelson, a real picture appeared in Vienna. The *Wiener Zeitung* on 26th March 1799 (No22, p.808) published the following announcement of the Arts and Music Publishing House of Artaria & Co.

> *Seeschlacht bei Abukir an der Mündung des Nils am 1., 2. und 3. August 1798. Gezeichnet nach dem Originale eines Augenzeugen auf der Nelsonschen Flotte von C. Schütz und gestochen von P. Peckenkam. - Dieses Blatt stellt von der in den Annalen der britischen Seesiege beispiellosen Schlacht bei Abukir eigentlich die schreckliche Szene des zweiten Tages vor in dem Moment, als der L'Orient auffliegt. Die Trümmer des französischen Admiralschiffes treiben am Vordergrunde herum. Man sieht die republikanischen Schiffe umrungen von den englischen und im hoffnungslosen Kampfe mit denselben. Einige haben bereits [die Segel] gestrichen und andere fliehen mit vollen Segeln. Sämtliche Schiffe beider Flotten sind auf dem Blatte mit Buchstaben bezeichnet und in der Aufschrift nach denselben benennet. In der Ferne sieht man Abukir und die Mündung des Nils. Der Preis ist schön illuminiert 3 fl. und braun gedruckt 2 fl.*

("Sea-battle of Aboukir at the mouth of the Nile on the 1st, 2nd and 3rd August 1798. Drawn after the original of an eyewitness in Nelson's fleet by C.Schütz and engraved by P. Peckenkam. This picture represents the battle of Aboukir unprecedented in the annals of British naval victories, more exactly, the dreadful scene of the second day at the moment when the *L'Orient* is blowing up. The wreckage of the French flag ship is drifting about in the foreground. One sees the Republican ships surrounded by the English in a hopeless struggle. Some have already struck [their flags] while others flee under full pressure of sail. In the painting all the ships of both fleets are marked with letters indicating their names which are given in the explanatory text. In the distance one sees Aboukir and the mouth of the Nile. The price is 3 fl, for a finely illuminated copy, and 2 fl. for a copy printed in brown." )

It is clear that Carl Schütz, a popular engraver of Viennese views, used an English model. Probably the original was not a painting at all, but the pamphlet which, although published anonymously, originated from the pen of Rear-Admiral Sir Edward Berry and contained a plan of the battle array (1st and 2nd of August): "An authentic Narrative of the Proceedings of His Majesty's Squadron, under the Command of Rear-Admiral Sir Horatio Nelson, from its Sailing from Gibraltar to the Conclusion of the glorious Battle of the Nile; drawn up from the Minutes of an Officer of Rank in the Squadron", London, printed for T. Cadell, etc. 1798.[19] The engraver's correct name is Peter Beckenkamp, of Cologne.

And now for the Nelson fashions: As early as 1799 *Der wiederaufgelebte Eipeldauer* (editor Joseph Richter), a periodical in popular taste, pro-Government and probably subsidised, and written in Viennese dialect, mentions bonnets *à la Nelson* and *à la Buonaparte;* this warrants the assumption that there might have been a political division in the feminine world of that day. The first mention of a Nelson fashion in the head-dress of Viennese ladies was made in the first issue of that periodical 1799-1801 series, first issue, p.47; the exact date is not indicated:

> *Jetzt tragen unsre Frauenzimmer neue Modehauben à la Nelson und à la Panaparti. Mein Frau Gemahlin, die jetzt zum Schein auf einmal ein Patriotin sein will, tragt jetzt auch ein Haube à la Nelson, und da sieht s'darin aus, wie ein Krokodil.*

("Our womenfolk now wear new fashionable bonnets *à la Nelson* and *à la Buonaparte.* My wife, who suddenly for the sake of fashion wants to appear a patriot, is now wearing a bonnet *à la Nelson*, and in it she looks like a crocodile".)

A footnote says: "the Nelson bonnet really looks like the head of a crocodile", which is perhaps an allusion to the Nile.

In 1800 the same periodical again has something to say about a Nelson fashion in the 18th issue, p.42:

> *Eine Menge tragn noch immer den Admiral Nelson aufn Leib, der ist aber jetzt um und um mit auszupften Franzeln besetzt, und da sieht man also jetzt, wo man nur hinschaut, solche auszupfte und ausgefranzelte Fraüln und gnädige Fraun.*

("A great many still wear the "Admiral Nelson" but it is now trimmed with little fringes, and so one can now see, wherever one looks, such befringed young maids and matrons.")

It seems therefore, that the Nelson Fashion had influenced other articles in ladies' clothing, even before our hero visited Vienna.

What then was the appearance of a lady dressed in this fashion? For a long time it seemed impossible to find an answer to this question. The author, however, was on the right track when he looked through the fashion prints of the late Dr August Heymann's private collection (now in the *Museum der Stadt Wien*) which were mostly taken from contemporary almanacs: for at that time a fashion magazine did not exist in Vienna. In this collection we found two small engravings of the year 1799, which we hoped would answer the question for us. One of the two half-length portraits shows a lady, facing to the right, wearing a quilted bonnet trimmed with a frill of ribbons and feathers, and with it a pair of circular earrings.

The other portrays a lady with short, curly hair, known on the Continent as *Tituskopf* and similar to the style adopted by Lady Hamilton in some of her portraits, with a ribbon in the hair, she wears no bonnet but her earrings are in the form of an anchor! These pictures were very tempting to use, but they were misleading. The number of almanacs published about 1800 is large, and a complete collection is nowhere to be found. The task seemed hopeless; chance, however, came to the rescue. At the sale by auction of the Vienna Collection of Franz Trau on April 2nd and 3rd 1935 (Gilhofer & Ranschburg, Vienna), lot no.486 was a series of the *Toilettenkalender für Frauenzimmer*,[20] published in Vienna by the bookbinder J.Grämmer. Its 20th volume, for the year 1801, was illustrated with copper plates by Clemens Kohl. On page 5, no. 10 of the costumes is an unsigned fashion picture of a figure, called "Nelson". So we have contemporary evidence of Nelson's popularity in Vienna at the time of his visit in the late summer of 1800, or shortly afterwards. (It is usual with almanacs as with calendars to publish them in the autumn of the preceding year.) This figure again wears a bonnet trimmed with ostrich feathers, leaving room for short curls. Frills seem to adorn the neckband but fringes can be discerned only at the hem of the high-girded Empire style dress. It will be seen that the Nelson Fashion in Vienna affected not only the head, but the entire figure.[21] At that time the attire of Lady Hamilton also may have had an influence on the new clothes,[22] as it is difficult to imagine that the Viennese fashion designers could have derived much inspiration for creations becoming to the fair sex from the uniform of the hero himself. Pezzl's anonymous *Skizze von Wien* (Sketch of Vienna)[23] refers as late as 1805 to a *Nelson Ueberrock* (Nelson Topcoat) which is said to have been worn in Vienna for some years: made of cashmere and *Halbtuch* (light cloth), first in dark blue and later in all colours; in summer it was also made in light silk and in winter in *ganzem Tuch* (full cloth).

Nelson received another great ovation in Vienna in 1799. It was an old custom in the summer months for great firework displays to be given in the *Prater*, the enormous pleasure grounds of the Viennese, a former hunting ground of the Court, in the fields between the Danube and the *Donaukanal*, which Joseph II had made over to the public. For almost a hundred years these fireworks were arranged by the Stuwer family, excellent technicians, who, however, were proverbially unlucky with the weather. It was a common saying in Vienna: "Whenever Stuwer announces fireworks, there will be rain." For that reason Johann Georg Stuwer, during this, his last season, gave alternative dates when he announced a firework display entitled "Nelson's Victory of Aboukir" for the 21st or 28th, May 1799 in the *Prater*, on the so-called *Feuerwerkswiese* (Fireworks field). They were the first main fireworks of that year, and the printed programme, 2 pages folio, still exists in the *Stadtbibliothek* of Vienna *(Feuerwerke, Schachtel I, 1799, No. I)*. The programme reads:

*Dienstag den 21. Mai oder (wenn es die Witterung nicht zulässt) den 28. Mai werde ich die Ehre haben, mein diesjährigen Erstes Feuerwerk abzubrennen, unter dem Titel: Nelsons Sieg bei Abukir. - Da voriges Jahr, als die Nachricht von Nelsons grossem Siege hier eintraf und die ganze Stadt mit Freude erfüllte, die Jahreszeit zu weit vorgerückt war, als dass es mir möglich gewesen wäre, diesen glänzenden Sieg mit einem angemessenen Feuerwerke zu feiern, so nehme ich ihn daher zum Stoffe meines diesjährigen ersten Feuerwerkes, das ich mit besonderem Fleisse und Eifer, und mit grossem Aufwande verfertiget habe, von dem einzigen Wunsch beseelet, dass es mir glücken möge, durch Plan und Ausführung mir auch dieses Jahr den gnädigen Beifall zu erwerben, womit das verehrte Publikum, seit so vielen Jahren, meine Bemühungen würdiget, ermuntert und belohnet. Den Anfang macht eine prächtige Brillant-Front, betitelt: Die ägyptische Sonnen-Spalier. Zusammensetzung, Abwechslung, Farbenspiel und anhaltendes Feuer werden diese Fronte jedem Kenner besonders empfehlen. - Zweite Fronte. Das Opferfeuer im Mars-Tempel. Hier erscheint eine perspektivische Zeichnung, in deren Mitte sich ein prächtiger architektonischer Tempel befindet. In diesem zeigt sich ein Opfertisch mit dem heiligen Feuer, das zur Kriegszeit dem Gotte Mars brennet. - Dritte Fronte. Die Brillant-Zeichnung à la Nelson. Diese ganz aus Funkelfeuer zusammengesetzte Zeichnungs-Fronte soll durch ihre Pracht, ihre Schönheit und ihre Grösse des grossen englischen Seehelden sich würdig zeigen.- Vierte Front. Die ägyptische Rose. Die sehr grosse, in allen ihren Teilen ganz bewegliche Brillant-Fronte wird dadurch umso sehenswürdiger, weil unter stets abwechselnden, mannigfaltigen, kunstreichen Bewegungen der Feuer-Maschinen, doch in der Mitte, immerfort eine gleichsam aus Edelsteinen zusammengesetzte ganz bewegliche Rose sich darstellet, deren*

*Schimmer gewiss allen Beifall finden wird - Hauptfronte. Nelsons*
*Sieg bei Abukir. Die Fronte, 432 Schuhe lang, stellet einen Theil des*
*mittelländischen Meeres vor: in einer Entfernung sieht man, nach*
*der Natur gezeichnet, die egyptische Küste, und auf derselben Abukir,*
*nebst einigen Gebirgen: rechts erscheint die englische Flotte, und*
*links, an der Mündung des Nils, die französische. Hierauf fängt von*
*beyden Seiten die Seeschlacht an. Über eine Weile nähern sich die*
*Englischen Schiffe den Französischen. Man sieht dann, wie von*
*letzteren das Admiralschiff, der Orient, in Brand gerält, und von den*
*Flammen verzehret wird. Nun ist der Sieg der Englischen Flotte*
*entschieden. Über derselben steigt die Fama empor, und schwinget*
*sich mit majestätischer Bewegung über die Afrikanischen Gewässer,*
*um nach Europa und England die Kundschaft von Nelsons grossem*
*Sieg zu bringen, Endlich kommt sie nach London, und nun entzündet*
*sich - Die Dekorazion, welche England sinnbildlich vorstellet, und*
*aus zu vielen Gegenständen bestehet, als dass sie hier umständlich*
*beschrieben werden könnte. Das darf ich jedoch zu derselben*
*Empfehlung zum voraus sagen, dass noch nie eine Dekorazion von*
*so prächtiger Zeichnung gesehen worden ist. Ich habe alle meine*
*Kräfte aufgebothen, um hier durch vereinigte Kunst, Pracht und*
*Neuheit den Beyfall des verehrten Publikums zu erwerben.*

("On Tuesday, May 21st, or (if the weather proves unfavourable) on May
28th, I shall have the honour of lighting my first fireworks of this year, under
the title: "Nelson's Victory at Aboukir." Last year, when the news of Nelson's
great victory was received and the whole city filled with joy, the season was too
far advanced and it was no longer possible for me to celebrate this brilliant
victory with an appropriate fireworks display, I take this, therefore, as the theme
of my first firework of this year, which I have constructed with particular
industry and eagerness and at great expense, animated by the sole desire of
being successful, in plan and execution, and of winning this year once again the
gracious applause with which the esteemed public, for so many years, honoured,
encouraged and rewarded my efforts. - A magnificent bouquet of fire constitutes
the first set-piece, entitled: "The Egyptian Sun *Espalier*". The composition,
variety, play of colours and the non-stop fire will especially commend this set-
piece to the connoisseur. - Second set-piece. "The sacrificial fire in the Temple
of Mars". Here a design in perspective appears, in the centre of which there is
a magnificent architectural temple. In this an altar can be seen with the holy fire
that burns when Mars is at war. - Third set-piece. "The brilliant design à la
Nelson." This set-piece, composed entirely of scintillating fire, should prove
itself worthy, in its splendour, beauty and magnitude, of the great English Naval
hero. - Fourth set-piece. "The Egyptian Rose". The very large and brilliant set-
piece is the more remarkable for the fact that while the firework is in constant,
and varied, artistic movement in all its parts, nevertheless in the centre there

*Maria Hermenegild, Princess Esterházy, born Princess Liechtenstein, was painted as a Sibyll in 1798 by Elisabeth Vigée-Le Brun.*

appears the unchanging representation of a moving rose, apparently formed of precious stones, the sparkle of which will surely meet with general appreciation.")

Only one other artistic event in connection with the Battle of the Nile has been noted before Nelson's arrival in Vienna. On June 19th 1800, the theatre in the Leopoldstadt produced a new military play, by Karl Friedrich Hensler, the theatre's own playright: *Heroine oder Die schöne Griechin in Alexandria* (Heroine, or the beautiful Greek girl of Alexandria)[24]. The play is directed against the French military rabble and represents the *Citoyens* as plunderers, murderers and libertines. What interests us in the play, however, is the fact that the news of Nelson's victory puts an end to their evil doings.

Let us now turn away from Vienna for a while to a note on Haydn, the Doctor of Music (hon. causa) of Oxford[25] who after 1790 displayed a particular affection for England, and who adapted so many Scottish, Irish and Welsh folksongs with such loving care. It concerns the so-called "Nelson Mass" and attempts to give its true history.

After the death of the first Prince Nikolaus Esterházy in 1790 and his own two journeys to England, Haydn was installed temporarily at the Princely Court in Eisenstadt. He usually lived during the summer and autumn months in his small house near the castle.[26] As part of his duties as court musician to the Prince Nikolaus II Esterházy he was required to provide every year a new Mass for the Saint's Day of the Prince's wife Maria Hermenegild Esterházy. The first of these was probably composed in 1796. On this Mass in C major he inscribed *In Tempore belli*, because at that time the French threatened Styria, a southern province of Austria. Since the Catholic Church after the death of Emperor Joseph II again sanctioned instrumental music, the six masses Haydn wrote in his late years are in full score. Most of them have been performed in the so-called *Bergkirche* Eisenstadt, a church of Pilgrimage.[27]

Haydn wrote his so-called *Nelson Messe* in the summer of 1798 in Eisenstadt. This Mass in D minor is probably the noblest of his works for the church. According to Haydn's own indication on the manuscript it was written between 10th July and 31st August, a time much shorter than he usually took to compose a work of this size. Haydn seems to have referred to this Mass, when towards the end of his life he told his biographer, Georg August Griesinger,[28] that only once had he completed a Mass "in one month, and only then because he had been unable to leave his house owing to illness". It is surprising that the manuscript of the Mass in D-minor[29] has neither title nor motto. It bears nothing but the pious formula *In nomine Domini* at the beginning and *Laus Deo* at the end.[30]     But Haydn in his so-called *Entwurf-Katalog* (Catalogue Sketch) describes his Mass as *Missa in Angustiis* (Mass for times of distress).[31] The other authentic catalogue of Haydn's works, of 1805, where it is listed as No.10 of the Masses, does not give a special title for this work. It was published by Breitkopf & Härtel in Leipzig in March 1803, as No. 3 of the Masses by Haydn, without any caption. The first vocal score, made by V. Novello and published in London in 1824, is also without a special title. A third edition (1850), which the same firm published in "The Three Favourite Masses, composed by Mozart, Haydn, and Beethoven", bears the inscription: "Haydn's Third (or Imperial) Mass". Similarly, the score which was published earlier by Porro in Paris about 1811 was called by the French title *L'Impériale*. This apocryphal name has been retained both in France and in England. The Mass, however, was not written for the coronation of an Austrian Emperor (as later Novello editions by calling it "Coronation Mass" would imply), nor was it written on the occasion of a Nelson victory,[32] and much less for Nelson himself, although since about 1805, in Vienna and all over Germany it has always been known as the "Nelson Mass". This, however, does not seem to be quite without reason. Tradition has it, that when Haydn was writing the "Benedictus" of this

*Joseph Haydn was at the pinnacle of his fame during his two visits to England. His portrait was painted and engraved in 1792 by Thomas Hardy.*

Mass, he received the news of Nelson's victory at Aboukir, that is to say before the end of August 1798, which inspired the sudden joyous chorus at the end of the "Benedictus" with its accompaniment of trumpets and drums suggesting, as it were, the entry of the heralds of victory.[33]  That the so-called Nelson Mass should have been given that name in 1800, because Haydn is said to have performed it at that time in Eisenstadt in the presence of Nelson himself, is dubious - as we shall see later.  Its first performance had already taken place in Eisenstadt in September 1798, not on September 8th, the day of the Virgin Mary's birth, nor on the following Sunday, the Saint's day of the Princess Maria Hermenegild Esterházy, but for unknown reasons on September 23rd.[34]  This is apparent from the notes in the diary of one Joseph Karl Rosenbaum:[35]

> Um 10 Uhr ging ich mit Carl in die grosse Kirche, wo das neue Amt von Haydn gemacht wurde.

("At 10 o'clock I went with Carl into the great church, where the new service by Haydn was given.")

It is remarkable in the history of this work (which in England, strangely enough, is not called the Nelson Mass) that Schubert conducted it on an Easter Sunday, April 4th 1820 in the *Altlerchenfelder-Kirche* in Vienna, where his brother Ferdinand was choirmaster at that time. In 1833, the Mass was performed at the unveiling of the new cross on the *Paulaner-Kirche* in the Wieden suburb of Vienna under Franz Glöggl.[36] In the summer of 1844 it was condemned as being too worldly after a repetition in the *Minoriten-Kirche* in Vienna. The critic Athanasius (nom de plume of Karl Magnus Gross)[37] went as far as to call the "Benedictus" a veritable military march with galloping cavalry; whereas this should have been naval music! Yet it was not Haydn's intention to depict either cavalry charges or naval battles in music.[38] Maybe he merely expressed his happiness over the English victory when he included trumpets and the roll of the drum in his Mass.[39] The gardeners of the Vienna suburb Erdberg had this Mass performed annually in the 19th century, as a thanksgiving for their sandy soil; in consequence it was also known locally as the *Mehlsand-Messe* ("Powdery Sand Mass").

As a point of interest it should here be mentioned, that the German title of the English "Haydn" song *Buonaparte oder Der Wanderer in Aegypten* ("Buonaparte or the wanderer in Egypt") is misleading. It is to be found in part two of the second series of "6 Original Canzonettas", which was published in London in 1796, with the title "The Wanderer". Both the text and the original music are the work of Dr. Henry Harington who dedicated the song to Haydn. Haydn changed the

*Entry of the trumpets 'a Tre unisoni' in the Benedictus from Haydn's so-called 'Nelson Mass'*

song slightly and later included it as his own composition in that collection.[40] The German text, by Daniel Jäger begins: *Wir wandern in Wüsten bei glühender Hitze* ("We wander in deserts mid glowing heat"). Thus the song was published in the middle of 1798 by Artaria & Co. in Vienna, as No.2 of part four of the series *Sechs Lieder* by Haydn.[41] It is clear that neither Haydn's nor Harington's original song had anything to do with Buonaparte in Egypt, nor, incidentally, with Nelson.

Near Eisenstadt in the vicinity of the large, but shallow Neusiedler-See, lies the town of Sopron, called in German Ödenburg.[42] Here was established the firm of Siess, who among other things printed the libretto for Haydn's opera *L'infedeltà delusa* in 1773, and the libretti for his operas *L'incontro improviso* in 1775 and *L'isola disabitata* in 1779. Here also they printed a Latin eulogy of Nelson, written by the retired cleric Joachim Hödl, who was born ca.1737 in Graz, the capital of Austrian Styria. He served as a missionary in Peru from 1754 until 1770; then when the Jesuit Order, to which he belonged, was dissolved, he ministered as a priest in Werschetz. This town lies between Temesvar and Belgrade and now belongs to Jugoslavia.[43] Later Hödl went to live in Ebreichsdorf, situated between Wiener Neustadt and Eisenstadt, or Wiener Neustadt and Ödenburg. In his numerous poems, written for special occasions in Latin or in a mixture of German and Latin, he calls himself *"Musa Verschetzensis"* or *"Ebreichsdorfensis"*.[44] Incidentally, it was the custom among educated men, just in Hungary at that time, to speak Latin; a means, no doubt of overcoming the language difficulties between the central administration in Vienna and the authorities beyond the *Leitha*. This Latin eulogy by Hödl, which is not dated, was badly printed as a booklet with loose covers, the only known copy of which is preserved in the National Museum in Budapest. It bears the title: *Nelsonis Anglicanis belliducis victoria navali pugna at Nili fluminis ostia calendis Augusti anni MDCCXCVIII reportata inclytae nationis Anglicanae honoribus ab Ebreichsdorfensi musa festivo elego decantata. Sopronii typis Annae Clarae Siess.* On the back of the title-page there are two distiches on Buonaparte and Nelson, and at the end of the poem the author gives his name and place of residence. The poem - with slight corrections - is printed in the Appendix of this book.

1 Lady Mary Wortley Montagu, who had met him in Vienna in 1716, compared him with Hercules at the Court of Omphale ("Letters", Second Edition, London, 1763, 1.118). Curiously enough, Helfert made the same comparison 150 years later when writing of Nelson.
2 It is true that the chancellor, Prince Kaunitz, exhibited in 1792 the portrait of the Lady, which Madame Vigée-Le Brun had brought to Vienna, in his Salon for two weeks. It is unlikely, however, that the Hamiltons visited Vienna in 1788 (1791 would be a more probable date).
3 Captain Thomas Bladen, who did not leave Egypt until the middle of August, brought the news to Naples on September the 3rd and then travelled via Vienna to London, where he arrived on October 2nd.
4 Also written Vanhal, now usually Wanhall.
5 Victory of the Austrian Archduke Charles over the French General Jourdan, September 3rd 1796.
6 A copy of the first edition (Joseph Eder & Co) is in the *Musiksammlung* of Dresden.
7 Cf. Eduard Hanslick's *Geschichte des Concertwesens in Wien,* Wien 1869, p.1 71; A.W.Thayer's "Beethoven", vol. III, 2nd Edition, Leipzig 1911, pp. 100 and 384 et seq.
8 These three words (the last one hardly legible) are printed in blue.
9 Vide: previous footnote.
10 As we know, this could not have taken place until the end of 1800.
11 "Rule Britannia" is quoted at this point.

12 The sixth son, and ninth child, of King George III.

13 As we know, Nelson captured these two ships in 1800.

14 An ironic review of Kauer's Nelson Music was published in the *Leipzig Allgemeine musikalische Zeitung* on April 22nd 1801.

15 Wanhall was only leader of the orchestra there.

16 The second was the *Freihaustheater,* where Mozart's "Magic Flute" was first performed, and the third is the still existing *Josefstädter Theater,* for the reopening of which after its restoration Beethoven wrote his overture, "The Consecration of the House".

17 Hammer, later Ritter von Purgstall, born in Graz 1774, became secretary and interpreter to Admiral Sir William Sidney Smith in 1779, and went himself to Alexandria with a British expedition.

18 An ode in Latin and German, signed by V. *Auf Nelson's Sieg bey Abukir* (On Nelson's Victory of Aboukir) had already appeared in the November number (pp.335-7).

19 First published in the "True Briton" and in the "Sun". At the end of 1798 it appeared separately, enlarged as a 2nd and 3rd edition. Another anonymous booklet was published in Constantinople, of which only a reprint without place of publication is known: *Relation de la bataille navale du Nil entre les flottes Anglaise et Française du 1.. au 3. Août,1798.*

20 Cf. Karl Goedeke, *Grundriss zur Geschichte der deutschen Literatur,* Leipzig 1898, vol.6, p. 515 (k); and *Katalog der Freiherrlich von Lipperheide'schen Kostümbibliothek,* Berlin 1905, vol.2, no.4480.

21 If A. Corbett-Smith says in his Nelson Book (London1926, p.242): "Soaps, dresses, hats and fichus were named after the pair", it is an exaggeration as far as Austria is concerned.

22 On September 8th (et. seq.) 1798, she had already written to Nelson from Naples (Walter Sichel, "Emma Lady Hamilton", p.488): "My dress from head to foot is alla Nelson. Ask [Captain] Hoste. Even my shawl is in blue with gold anchors all over. My earrings are Nelson's anchors; in short, we are beNelsoned all over."

23 No. 1, pp.97 et. seq.

24 Cf. Egon con Komorczynski in the *Jahrbuch der Grillparter Gesellschaft,* Vienna 1913, Vol.24, pp. 158 et.seq.

25 In 1802 Nelson and Sir William Hamilton were made Doctors of Law at Oxford.

26 During his last years Haydn regularly spent the winter and spring in his own house in a suburb of Vienna, where he also died and which is now the Haydn Museum.

27 His remains rested under the organ of this church until 1820 when an English admirer influenced Prince Esterházy to have them removed from Vienna. Adolphus Frederick Duke of Cambridge, on a visit to Eisenstadt, observed in a toast given at a dinner held after a performance of the "Creation", that the Esterházys should be happy having Haydn near them in death as in life (Pohl-Botstiber, Leipzig 1927), ("Haydn", III.283).

28 *"Biographische Notizen",* p.116.

29 *Nationalbibliothek,* Vienna, Cod. 16478.

30 Haydn also used this invocation and ejaculation on his secular manuscripts.

31 See Carl Maria Brand's *Die Messen Joseph Haydns,* Würzburg 1941, and the facsimile editions of Haydn's Catalogues by Jens Peter Larsen, Copenhagen 1941.

32 Later it was even associated with Nelson's victory of Trafalgar (1805).

33 As the news of the battle did not reach Naples until September 3rd, it is unlikely that the result was known at Eisenstadt in August.

34 Such masses were usually performed in the chapel of the castle and sometimes repeated in the hall (the *Sala terrena).* This time, however, the first performance seems to have taken place in the parish church St Martin.

35 Rosenbaum, secretary to Count Karl Esterházy, later married the opera singer Theresa Gassmann, a friend of Haydn's. His diary is preserved in the *Nationalbibliothek,* Vienna (published by E. Radant in Haydn - Yearbook V, 1967: Editorial note).

36 Cf. "The Harmonicon", London 1833, p.389.

37 *Allgemeine Wiener Musikzeitung,* vol.4 p.389.

38 Here it should be pointed out, that when in London in 1794 Haydn wrote an "Invocation of Neptune" the manuscript of which is in the British Museum. (Vide Haydn's English diaries, Griesinger's *Biographische Notizen,* and Pohl-Botstiber's "Haydn", III, 84 and 92). This hymn on the "Sovereignty of the Sea" had already been composed three times. Haydn's composition remained unfinished; only one aria for Bass with the ensuing chorus exists.

39 Actually, the Mass of 1796 is called the *Paukenmesse* (Mass with Drums) because in the *Agnus* the Drums are introduced.

40 Cf. The *Suleika-Gesänge (Westwind* and *Ostwind)* by Marianne Willemer in Goethe's *Westöstlicher Divan.*

41 Cf. Pohl-Botstiber "Haydn", III.223 and 327 (not quite correct).

42 At the time Eisenstadt (Kismarton) and Sopron were situated in Hungary; now the Austro-Hungarian frontier runs between the towns.

43 Today Visac (Editorial note).

44 Vide J.N. Stöger, *Scriptores Austriacae Societatis Jesu,* 1856, p.144; C. von Wurzbach, *Biographisches Lexicon des Kaisertums Oesterreich,* Vienna 1863, IX. 93; Geza Petrik, *Magyarország bibliográfiája* 1711-1867, II, 176,; and K. Goedeke, *Grundriss zur Geschichte der deutschen Literatur,* Vol.VI, pp.634 et. seq. (No.11).

# CHAPTER 7
## Nelson and the Hamiltons in Austria and Hungary

### Arrival in Austria

Nelson set foot on Imperial territory on 1st August 1800, in Trieste, the former Austrian port (now part of Italy). To describe his arrival with his party and his journey northwards we shall quote one of the two Hungarian newspapers, which appeared at that time in Vienna, the "Magyar Hírmondó" (Hungarian News-Messenger), which on August 1st 1800 brought news of July 18th from Florence: "On the morning of the 12th, Her Majesty the Queen of Naples arrived here from Livorno with her son and three daughters. She was accompanied by Cardinal Ruffo and the English Rear-Admiral Nelson, the commander of the ships which had carried Her Majesty from Palermo, the capital of Sicily, to Livorno. Her Majesty stayed at the Palazzo Pitti. On July

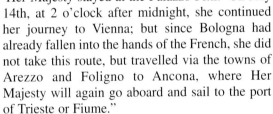

14th, at 2 o'clock after midnight, she continued her journey to Vienna; but since Bologna had already fallen into the hands of the French, she did not take this route, but travelled via the towns of Arezzo and Foligno to Ancona, where Her Majesty will again go aboard and sail to the port of Trieste or Fiume."

Also a local newspaper, "L'Osservatore Triestimo" reports on 4th[1] and 8th August 1800. The second report, as Carlo L. Curiel epitomizes it in his book *Il Teatro S. Pietro di Trieste, 1690 - 1801*, reads:[2]

*"Vi fu una volontaria publica illuminazione notturna, che causa il forte ed ostinato vento venne differita di sera fino al 10. L'edificio dei Tribunali, la gran Guardia, la Loggia, la facciata della Chiesa di S.Pietro, della Biblioteca, del Teatro e delle case sulla Piazza, le colonne, la fontana, la Torre dell 'Orologio comparvero*

*View of the town and port of Trieste. The Queen of Naples, accompanied by Lord Nelson, Lord and Lady Hamilton, landed here on 1 August 1800, eventually travelling through Laibach and Graz to Vienna.*

*arricchiti di moltitudine di lumi a cera, a olio, a transparenti, disposti in forma allusiva al Regio nome della M.S., e sprapassanti il numero di 4 mila." "Vi fu gioia dell'esultante popolazione", enumera ancora la gazetta, "ricevimento del Governatore, del general maggiore de Köbles, del barone Pittoni, del Vescovo e Capitolo, della Deputazione di Borsa; la Regina, dopo essersi compiaciuta di mostrarsi piena di affabilità e cortesia per ben due volte in Teatro all'affezionato Publico che da per tutto replicatamente l'acclamava, a proseguito con la Regia Prole e Corte, circa la mezza-notte di jeri 10 del corrente il suo viaggio alla volta di Vienna."*

("There was a "voluntary public night illumination", which, because of the strong and obstinate wind, was postponed from the evening until the 10th. in the evening. The building of the Tribunals, the Main Guardhouse, the *Loggia*, the façade of the Church of St. Peter's, of the library, the theatre and the houses of the square, the columns, the fountain, the Clock Tower, were enriched by a multitude of more than four thousand wax lights, oil lamps, and transparencies, arranged in a way suggestive of the Royal name of H.M." "There was joy among the exultant population", the newspaper goes on to relate; "the Queen received the Governor, Major-General de Köbles, Baron Pittoni, the Bishop and Chapter, and a deputation from the Bourse; after having been graciously pleased to show herself on two occasions where she was full of affability and courtesy to the affectionate public which from all sides acclaimed her repeatedly, she continued her journey to Vienna with her Royal children and the Court, about midnight of yesterday, the 10th").

We have further descriptions from other reports. James Harrison, who got his information from Lady Hamilton, writes:[3] "They arrived there [at Trieste] on the 1st of August 1800,[4] being the second anniversary of his lordship's glorious victory of the Nile. At this, as well as every other place, they were received with universal rejoicings, and experienced every mark of honour; but the Queen and Sir William Hamilton had both caught violent colds on board the Russian ship, followed by a dangerous degree of fever, which confined them upwards of a fortnight, and considerably alarmed their friends. From Trieste, the Queen immediately on her recovery, departed for Vienna; and Lord Nelson, with Sir William and Lady Hamilton two days afterwards, accompanied by Mr. Anderson, the British Vice-Consul,[5] who offered his services in conducting them there, being perfectly familiar with that particular route through the province of Carniola, Carinthia, Stiria and into [Inner] Austria." Harrison adds on p.251: "... even the barriers, like our turnpikes, were all thrown open on his [Nelson's] approach, and the whole company, sanctioned by the hero's presence, permitted gratuitously to pass."

We have yet to quote another traveller on that journey, Miss Knight, who wrote to Sir Edward Berry on August 9th from Trieste:[6]

"Poor Sir William Hamilton has been so ill that the physicians had almost given him up: he is now better, and I hope we shall be able to set off to-morrow night for Vienna. The Queen and thirty-four of her suite have had fevers: you can form no idea of the helplessness of the party ... He [Lord Nelson] is followed by thousands when he goes out, and for the illumination that is to take place this evening, there are many "Viva Nelson!" prepared." The Queen eventually left for Vienna on August 10th, but Nelson had to remain in Trieste another two days on account of Sir William Hamilton's indisposition.

We can follow the second, or rather the third, group of travellers[7] along their journey. On August 14th Nelson and the Hamiltons, Mrs. Cadogan and Miss Knight - and apparently the Vice-Consul Anderson - arrived in Laibach.[8] A Philharmonic Society had existed in Laibach for many years, indeed it was one of the oldest in existence. In his history of this society, Dr Fr. Keesbacher records on August 14th 1800:[9]

> Die Gesellschaft veranstaltete eine Akademie zu Ehren der Anwesenheit Nelsons, des Lords vom Nil und Siegers von Abukir. Dieser nun besuchte dieselbe, in Gesellschaft des Milord und Milady Hamilton und äusserte sich sehr wohlgefällig über die Leistungen der Dilettanten. Die berühmte, in England verfertigte Schlachtsinfonie machte den Anfang des Konzertes. Hierauf wurde die italienische Arie: La virtù brittanna "mit ausnehmenden Gefühl und Pünktlichkeit" vorgetragen. Diese und alle übrigen ausgeführten Stücke, erhöhten den frohen Sinn.

("The Society organized a musical soirée in honour of the presence of Nelson, Lord of the Nile, and Victor of Aboukir. He attended the same, accompanied by Milord and Milady Hamilton, and expressed himself very favourably on the achievements of the amateurs. The concert opened with the famous battle symphony, written in England. Then the Aria: La virtù brittanna (British Virtue) was performed "with exceptional feeling and precision". These and all other items which were performed, heightened the gay atmosphere of the occasion").

Keesbacher, who bases his report on old records of the Society, refers to Haydn, when he speaks of the unnamed composer of the symphony, who had become the first honorary member of the Laibach Philharmonic Society shortly before this. By the "battle-symphony" we understand he refers to the Military Symphony, one of the twelve London Symphonies by the master, which had become so popular in England and which was written during his second stay in this country in 1794. The Italian Aria was probably Handel's Arioso from his opera "Teseo" (Act 4, Scene 6) which -adapted to English words - was printed in the same month, August 1800, in "The Lady's Magazine" under the title: "Virtue" (Chi ritorna alia mia mente...)

The journey by coach proceeded via Klagenfurt, the capital of Carinthia, to Graz in Styria. Of their stay in Graz the official Grätzer Zeitung reports on August 18th:

*"Den 15.d. abends acht Uhr kam endlich, lange erwartet, die dritte Abteilung der königlich neapolitanischen Reisegesellschaft an. Sie enthielt den gewesenen königlich gross britanischen Gesandten am neapolitanischen Hofe, Lord Hamilton samt seiner Frau Gemahlin und den Sieger am Nil (Abukir) Admiral Nelson. Sie stiegen ebenfalls im Schmelzerischen Gasthof ab, wo Nelson von dem zahlreich versammelten Volke mit lautem Vivatgeschrei bewillkommt wurde.*

*Diese Aufmerksamkeit des Publikums und dessen Hochachtungs- und Zuneigungsbezeigungen rührten den Helden so sehr, dass er nicht nur einem grossen Teil desselben den Zutritt in sein Zimmer gestattete, sondern sogar - die schöne Lady Hamilton am Arme - auf die Gasse unter das Volk trat, und auf diese Art die Begierde desselben, ihn zu sehen, auf das gefälligste befriedigte. Man fand, dass die Porträts, die man von ihm hat, ihm so ziemlich ähnlich sehen. Er ist von kleinem Körperbau, blassem und eingefallenem Angesicht, in das Gesicht gekämmten Haaren. Den Verlust eines Auges bemerkt man nicht so sehr, als den des rechten Armes, da er keine Maschine trägt, sondern den leeren Ärmel an den zusammengeschlossenen Rock angeheftet hat. Neben der Hochachtung, die der Held allgemein einflösste, erregte die Schönheit der Lady Hamilton ebensoviele Bewunderung. Bei diesen Eindrücken übersah man jedoch eine junge Mohrin von beiläufig 17 Jahren nicht, welche die vierte Person in dem Wagen des Lords ausmachte und für ein Gegenstück einer schwarzen Schönheit zu den erhabenen Reizen der Lady Hamilton gelten konnte. Diese ganze Kolonne trat den 16. morgens um 4 Uhr ihre weitere Reise von hier nach Wien an".*

("On the 15th inst. at 8 o'clock in the evening, there arrived at long last the third party of Royal Neapolitan travellers. It comprised the ex-ambassador of Great Britain to the Neapolitan Court, Lord Hamilton, together with his wife, and the Victor of the Nile (Aboukir), Admiral Nelson. They too [like the Queen before them] stayed at *Schmelzer's Gasthof* [10] where Nelson was greeted with loud cheers by the people who had gathered in great numbers to welcome him. This attention on the part of the public and its manifestation of esteem and affection moved the hero to such an extent, that he not only admitted a large number to his room, but even went into the street among the people - with the beautiful Lady Hamilton on his arm - and thus most kindly satisfied their desire to see him. It was found that the portraits one has of him bear a fair likeness. He is of small, slight build, his face is pale and sunk, with the hair combed on to the forehead; the loss of an eye is less noticeable than that of the right arm, as he does not wear an artificial limb but fastens the empty sleeve across his buttoned tunic. The respect which the hero universally inspired was equalled by the admiration for Lady Hamilton's beauty. Despite these impressions, a young coloured girl of about 17, who was the fourth passenger in the carriage of his Lordship and who was a counterpart in black beauty of Lady Hamilton's noble charms, did not pass unnoticed. On 16th at 4 a.m. the whole party proceeded on its journey from here to Vienna.")

This party, which, as we see, included a young coloured girl[11], probably consisted of more than 15 persons and therefore travelled in several coaches. Mrs. Cadogan and Miss Knight occupied the second coach, presumably with Mr. Anderson. The journey proceeded via Bruck an der Mur over the Semmering Pass to Wiener Neustadt, where they arrived on the 17th, supping and staying the night at the *Zum Hirschen* inn. Here the party came to the notice of Count Karl Zinzendorf, then Governor of Lower Austria who had just returned from a visit to the Austrian headquarters of the *Deutsche Ritterorden* (German Order of Knighthood) of which he was provincial Commander. He had come to Wiener Neustadt by a different route. He eventually arrived in Vienna on the same day as Nelson. In the Count's diary of sixty volumes,[12] which is of special significance for the history of music, he made this entry on 18th August: *"Le Prince Albani y vint qui me dit que Nelson et Hamilton sont partis à 4 h du matin.* (Prince Albani came and told me that Nelson and Hamilton left at 4 o'clock in the morning").

The journey proceeded via Baden to Vienna where the party arrived on the same day, Monday, 18th August, four days after Queen Maria Carolina. The Queen had already settled down, having arrived with her children to find her large suite at Schönbrunn Palace[13] on the 14th at 10 o'clock in the evening; she stayed for about a year.

The Emperor and Empress, accompanied by the exiled Grand Duke Ferdinand III of Tuscany (in Vienna since April 1799), had left Schönbrunn to meet the Queen at Schottwien. They proposed giving a *Cercle* for her at the Imperial Palace in the City on August 17th, but the health of the Queen made it necessary to postpone this official reception for a week, so that all the visitors could be welcomed on the same occasion.

---

1 In the first report, Nelson and the Hamiltons are mentioned among the Queen's escort.

2 Milano 1937, pp.359 et. seq.

3 "The Life of the Right Honorable Horatio Lord Viscount Nelson", London 1806, II. 294 et. seq.

4 Miss Knight in her "Autobiography", I. 151f. , erroneously writes 2nd August. The *Wiener Zeitung* of 13th August (No.65, p.2593) expressly states: *am 1. abends um 8 Uhr* (on the 1st, at 8 p.m.).

5 The Consul was Edward Stanley.

6 "The Dispatches and Letters of ... Nelson", IV. 265. A letter by Nelson himself written to his wife from Trieste, seems to be lost.

7 While the two travelling relays of the Queen required 36 and 46 post-horses respectively to cover the journey in six days, Nelson's party needed only 25, but took 8 days to reach Vienna.

8 Then the capital of the Austrian province of Krain (now, as Ljubljana, capital of Slovenia, editorial note).

9 *Die Philharmonische Gesellschaft in Laibach seit dem Jahre ihrer Gründung 1702 bis zu ihrer Umgestaltung 1862*, Leipzig 1862, p.30. There the concert is erroneously dated 1797.

10 An inn near the new bridge across the Mur, later called the *Erzherzog Johann* Hotel.

11 Possibly waiting on Lady Hamilton and perhaps a gift from Nelson.

12 Preserved in the *Haus-, Hof- und Staatsarchiv,* Vienna.

13 The summer residence of the Austrian Court.

*The Graben in Vienna, engraved by Passini after a painting by G C Wilder. On the extreme right is the guest house where Nelson and his friends stayed.*

# CHAPTER 8
## *In Vienna*

In Vienna Nelson and the Hamiltons stayed in the *Graben*. This, the largest square in the city, is really a broad street, between St. Stephen's Cathedral and the Imperial Palace. *Der Graben* (the Moat), once situated outside the oldest part of the town and long before filled in, was the centre of traffic, especially for those who went shopping or sightseeing. In the middle of the *Graben* stands the marble column commemorating the plague, and (at that time) at each end stood a fountain. Near the fountains lemonade stalls were erected and here in the evenings, musical serenades were sometimes improvised. By night this was the meeting place of easy-going "Nymphs", but in the daytime, the *Graben* had a dignity of its own and offered a beautiful and harmonious picture with its old patrician houses and many vaulted shops, each with its differently shaped

entrances and shop-windows. On the north side, near St. Stephen's Cathedral, stood the magnificent *Trattnerhof,* the house of the printer von Trattner.[1] The great *Grabenhof* and other stately houses added dignity and grandeur to the south side of the *Graben.* From there the *Habsburgergasse* (of today) forks off to the south, as the last side-street before the *Kohlmarkt* (Coal Market) going towards the Imperial Palace. While the *Grabenhof* stood on the left corner of the *Habsburgergasse,* nearer the Plague Column, the house with which we are now concerned, was situated on the right hand corner of this side-street, nearer the *Kohlmarkt.*

It was called the *Gasthof aller Biedermänner* (The Inn of all Honest Men), a long forgotten small hotel. We recognise it in the right foreground on the view of the *Graben,* which Johann Nepomuk Passini engraved about 1820, after Georg Christoph Wilder.[2] In this picture, which shows us the whole square from west to east, one can see the *Grabenhof* (on the right) much more clearly than our little inn, only a part of which, unfortunately, is visible. However, one can recognise the shop on the ground floor, the balcony on the first floor and the three upper storeys of the richly decorated façade, and on the corner below the roof one may discern a gargoyle in the form of an animal. The symbolic sign-board of the shop can also be seen. Under the broad balcony (a glass-covered veranda) on the first floor, there was probably a door, and above the balcony stood a charming baroque Madonna, whose picture has by chance been preserved. From the photographic detail of the house we can clearly see that the Madonna stood in a niche between the window of the second upper storey. The photograph by A. Stauda was taken about 1870; it shows modernised windows and is somewhat disfigured by telephone wires. Other photographs show the entire front and the corner, but do not show the balcony. An earlier photograph, by G. Grail, shows the corner and the balcony. There is also a photographic reproduction of the house, by J. Löwy, in *Neubauten und Concurrenzen in Oesterreich und Ungarn,* edited by Bresler.[3] This was made at the time of its demolition. On the slightly projecting ground floor there were three porches. The number of the house has changed many times. First it was No. 1175, then it became No. 1144 of the Inner City, and later No. 17, finally No. 16 of the *Graben.* Its original name was the *Prathaus,* more correctly *Brothaus* (bread house); it was later called *Zum deutschen Ritter* (The German Knight) and for a long time belonged to the Vienna Town Hospital.[4] At one period it was a tavern, gambling house and dancing place, whose reputation was not of the very best. During the sixteenth and seventeenth centuries the house was privately owned, and it is probable that about 1725 it was restored to the shape which it more or less retained in the nineteenth century. At the end of the eighteenth century it served as an inn for the French cook, Anton Villar, who is mentioned by Michael Kelly.[5] Kelly had just made the acquaintance of his compatriot, Dr O'Rourke, and the pedestrian traveller John Stewart ("Walking Stewart"). Of this occasion he writes:

"After taking our punch, we separated, and agreed to meet and dine together the next day at the French house, kept by the famous Monsieur Villar, celebrated, though a Frenchman, for giving excellent beef steaks, and dressing them to perfection à l'Anglaise... He [Stewart] was a great enthusiast about music although not about beef steaks; for, of the most tender, and dressed in Monsieur Villar's best manner, he would not touch a morsel; he lived entirely upon vegetables: but my friend, the Irish doctor, was in truth a beef-eater."

Somewhat later, Madame Theresia Villar is mentioned as hostess.[6] In 1800 her son, Johann Baptist, was running the establishment.[7] It was still referred to in 1805 as the inn of the Villar family.[8]

The *Eipeldauer Briefe*, the journal which later also published a view of the inn,[9] wrote in 1800:[10]

> *"Der grosse admirable Admiral Nelson ist auch z'Wien ankommen, und da stehn ein Menge Leut aufn Graben, die den tapferen Helden sehen wolln, und eine Menge Fraunzimmer wolln jetzt kein anders Kleid als ihren Nelson tragen, um ihm nur recht viel Ehr zu machen."*

("The great and admirable Admiral Nelson has also come to Vienna, and now crowds stand on the *Graben*, wishing to see the brave hero, and lots of women now refuse to wear any dress other than their 'Nelson', just to show him the greatest honour"). We see therefore that to the bonnet of 1798 has been added a robe, and in the 20th part, 1st letter p.13 we read:

> *Der berühmte Admiral Nelson ist noch immer z'Wien, und weil er im Gasthaus der Biedermänner wohnt, so stehn auch den ganzen Tag eine Menge Biedermänner vorn Haus und gucken auf d'Althone hinauf. Wie ich hör, so solls ihm z'Wien recht gut gfalln: er soll auch ein grosser Liebhaber von lustigen Komödien seyn, und da soll besonders der Kasperl und der Dadedl durch ihr spassiges Spiel grosse Ehr bey ihm eingelegt habn."*

(" The famous Admiral Nelson is still in Vienna, and because he is staying in the 'Inn of Honest Men', lots of honest men stand in front of the house all day long staring up at the balcony.[11] I hear that he is quite pleased with his stay in Vienna: he is also said to be a great lover of gay comedies and especially *Kasperl* and *Dadedl* are said to have won his great admiration with their merry antics." (About the *Kasperl* see below).

These two passages were known to C. F. Pohl, the great Haydn biographer, which led him and Hugo Botstiber, who completed Pohl's work,[12] to the assumption that Nelson had been in Vienna once before - in the spring of 1800 on a journey to Trieste - and that he returned in the late summer.[13] Botstiber suggests the first passage was written in April and the second in May, although the *Eipeldauer Briefe*[14] had already published an account of the Festival of St. Anne in Vienna, which fell on July 26th. In fact, the two quotations were written in the succeeding months of 1800.[15]

The first day that Nelson and the Hamiltons spent in Vienna, August 19th, was very hot,[16] and the heat persisted for a long time. This makes plausible the excuse that Sir William, during the first part of his visit, had to keep to his room at the inn, and it was for this reason that he allowed his wife to go about alone with Nelson. Be that as it may, she was regarded in Central Europe, at that time, as the unconsecrated consort of an uncrowned potentate, in which fashion Nelson was everywhere received. This was due not only to Lady Hamilton's condition which dated from the spring, but also because the hero had for so long accepted her loving care and her practical help in overcoming the handicap of his lost arm. To this was added her introduction by the Queen of Naples which, at least in Austria, made Emma acceptable to the Court. The Viennese, with their romantic leanings, found a couple after their own hearts in the unlawful partnership of the small wounded man who had defeated Napoleon and was yet so affable, and his charming companion. They certainly understood the position of the old knight in the background, because such tolerance was natural in Austria.

Nelson's first calls were, no doubt, on the English Ambassador, Lord Minto, at his office in town and on the Ambassador's wife in St.Veit. Soon after his visit Lady Minto wrote to her sister:[17] "You can have no notion of the anxiety and curiosity to see him [Nelson]. The door of his house is always crowded with people, and even the street, whenever his carriage is at the door;[18] and when he went to the play he was applauded, a thing which rarely happens here. On the road it was the same. The common people brought their children to touch him. One he took up in his arms, and when he gave it back to the mother she cried for joy, and said it would be lucky through life. I don't think him altered in the least. He has the same shock head, and the same honest simple manners; but he is devoted to Emma; he thinks her quite an angel and talks of her as such to her face and behind her back, and she leads him about like a keeper with a bear. She must sit by him at dinner to cut his meat;[19] and he carries her pocket handkerchief. The *aigrette* the Grand Signor [the Sultan] gave him is very ugly and not valuable, being rose diamonds. The crescent which he wears with the order is very handsome, but he is a gig from ribands, orders and stars. He is just the same with us as ever he was; says he owes everything to Lord Minto; that but for the 'interest he took about him he should have had no reward for his services in the first action, nor have been placed in a situation to obtain the second'."

In the evening of Tuesday, August 19th, Nelson and Lady Hamilton visited the *Hofburg-Theater* which was situated at that time in the old left wing of the *Hofburg* gate.[20] On that day Rosenbaum wrote in his journal: *Abends sang T - im B.Th. [Burgtheater] Griselda, ich ging hinein ... Im B.Th. war Nelson und Hamilton mit der Frau.*

("In the evening T-[Teresa, his young wife] sang in 'Griselda' at the Imperial Palace Theatre, I went . . . Nelson and Hamilton with wife were there.")

*The old Burgtheater in Vienna, where at that time opera was still performed. Nelson preferred the Kasperl-Theater in the Leopoldstadt.*

This was a performance of Nicola Piccinni's musical drama in two acts: "Griselda", text by Anelli after Boccaccio. Since 1794 this opera had been given alternately in the two Court theatres, the *Kärntnertor-Theater* and the *Burgtheater.* Incidentally, in 1798 the same text was used by the composer Paër, and his opera which he called *La Virtù al Cimento* (The Test of Virtue) also was included in the repertory of the two Court theatres in 1799. (In 1809, during the French occupation, Paër's opera was performed under the title "Griselda".)

On Thursday evening, August 21st, Nelson and the Hamiltons paid their respects to the Empress in Schönbrunn, and on the following day Nelson wrote to Lord Minto:[21] "Friday morning, Vienna, August 22nd, 1800 - My dear Lord, - Many thanks for your kind note of this morning. We will settle the place of our meeting when we meet at dinner: the time is not the best chosen for either of us. The Queen of Naples has desired anxiously Lady Hamilton to bring you to her this afternoon. The Empress would see us yesterday evening, and we had

*Lady Hamilton, after a French engraving by Manrin, depicting her as she must have appeared during her stay in Vienna with Lord Nelson.*

the noise of five fine healthy children[22] for an hour. With all our best wishes to you and Lady Minto, believe me, my dear Lord, as ever, your truly obliged and affectionate, - Bronte Nelson of the Nile."

On the evening of the same day, Nelson and Lady Hamilton were at the *Leopoldstädter Theater* in the *Praterstrasse* (at that time called *Jägerzeile*). We have learned earlier from the *Eipeldauer Briefe,* that our hero enjoyed the astute *Kasperl* and his clumsy partner, the *Thaddädel. Kasperl Larifari* - to give him his full name - was a stage character created in that theatre, which was popular in Vienna at that time. The *Leopoldstädter Theater* for this reason was often known as the *Kasperl-Theater*. The creator and unsurpassed actor of this character was Johann Laroche, whom Nelson saw repeatedly. Kasperl represented a merry naive peasant lad, a younger counterpart of the North German Hanswurst and the Italian Arlecchino, but more harmless and respectable than those two rogues. His costume was not as colourful as theirs; a red patch on the breast of the tunic, in the shape of a heart, was the sole emblem of his type, which remained unchanged in all the plays in which he appeared. Although long since banished from the stage, he is still alive to-day in all German-speaking countries, a well known, merry personality of the puppet stage. The modern version of Kasperl, with the hunchback, is to be found at fairs, and particularly at the Vienna *Wurstelprater* (the fun fair of the *Prater*), which derives its name from Hanswurst. The puppet show for little children, in which he appears, together with the merry-go-round forms the main attraction of the *Wurstelprater*.[23] The nearby *Kasperl-Theater* for adults had another comic character in Nelson's time, the *Thaddädel*, created by Anton Hasenhut. He was usually represented as a journeyman or an apprentice, greedy, foolish, fainthearted, and stupid, but always meddlesome and rather young.[24] In Mozart's time Kasperl had found a certain keen competitor, in the *Freihaus-Theater*, in Schikaneder's *Der dumme Anton aus dem Gebirge* ('The Silly Antony from the Mountains'). In Nestroy's days, *Kasperl* and *Thaddädel* were succeeded by the characters which this great satirical writer invented and acted himself, together with his portly colleague Scholz, in the same theatre in the Leopoldstadt.

The first conductor of this theatre, the highly gifted composer of musical plays Wenzel Müller (of whom several arias have become veritable folksongs), kept an accurate diary of all events connected with this stage for about fifty years. From this journal[25] we have already learned that Kauer produced his *Nelson- Schlacht* (Nelson battle) on December 23rd, 1798, at his annual benefit concert before Christmas. Here we find this entry:

*August 1800, 22. Ferrandino 1ter Theil, war der Admiral Nelson hier im Theater mit der Gräfin Hamilton.*

("On August 1800, 22. Ferrandino 1st part, Admiral Nelson was present in the theatre with Lady Hamilton").

This musical play, in three acts, is a continuation of the story of the robber-chief Rinaldini, adapted for Marinelli's[26] stage by Hensler, and it was not included in the repertory until August 14th.[27] Hensler's "Rinaldo Rinaldini" - dramatised after the novel by Goethe's brother-in-law, Vulpius, appeared at the end of 1799, and the second part of "Ferrandino" followed in the middle of 1801.

On August 23rd, the day after his visit at the *Leopoldstädter Theater*, Nelson was received alone in audience by the Emperor Franz - in the Imperial Palace, for this was an official occasion.[28] On Sunday the 24th, at noon, followed the postponed *Cercle* in the Palace, which was now given not only for the Queen of

Naples, but for Nelson and Lady Hamilton as well. Of this *Cercle* the *Protocollum aulicum in Ceremonialibus de Anno 1800*[29] reports:

> *August. Den 24t, war der von S<sup>er</sup> Majestät dem Kaiser bey Hofe in [der] kais. kön. Burg angeordnete Cercle. bey welchem die kais. königl. und königl. neapolitanische Familie, wie auch des Churfürsten von Kölln Maximilian und des Herzogs Albrecht von Sachsen-Teschen königl. Hoheiten, der englische Admiral Lord Nelson, welcher schon tags vorher bei Seiner Majestät dem Kaiser eine besondere Audienz hatte, und die Lady Hamilton erschienen. Bey dieser Gelegenheit wurden der Königinn von Neapel Majestät auch viele Fremde vorgestellt.- Nach geendigtem Cercle haben Ihre Majestäten der Kaiser und die Kaiserinn, wie auch der Königinn von Neapel Maj. mit Allerhöchster Familie das Mittagsmahl bey Sr. königl. Hoheit dem Herzoge Albrecht von Sachsen -Teschen im Augarten Hofgebäude eingenommen.*

("August, the 24th. The Cercle appointed by His Majesty the Emperor was held at the Court of Their Majesties in the Palace, which was attended by Their Majesties and the Royal Neapolitan family, also by the H.R.H. the Elector of Cologne, Maximilian[30] and H.R.H. Duke Albrecht of Sachsen-Teschen; there were also present the English Admiral Nelson, who had already on the previous day been admitted to a special audience by H.M. the Emperor, and Lady Hamilton. On this occasion many strangers were introduced to the Queen of Naples. When the *Cercle* was over, their Majesties the Emperor and the Empress, as well as the Queen of Naples with the Royal family took their lunch with H.R.M. the Duke Albrecht of Sachsen-Teschen in the *Augarten* Palace.")

The *Augarten*, situated in the suburb of Leopoldstadt, not far from the *Prater*, which was also opened to the public by the Emperor Joseph II, comprised an Imperial Palace, the old "Favorita", which had been destroyed during the second siege of Vienna by the Turks, after which it was rebuilt and used occasionally as a residence for members of the Habsburg family. Sometimes it was a restaurant where on spring mornings open air concerts were given.[31]

On August 27th[32] the *Wiener Zeitung* published a report similar to that in the *Protocollum aulicum*. On August 26th we read in the *Magyar Kurir*, the other Hungarian newspaper which appeared in Vienna,[33] that Nelson and Lady Hamilton were also present at this luncheon party, given by the Duke Albrecht of Sachsen-Teschen, uncle of the Emperor, together with Dukes Alexander and Ferdinand Friedrich of Württemberg, and 50 more persons. The Hungarian paper, more explicit than the Austrian official organ, affirms that "Admiral Nelson was present as was Sir William Hamilton...accompanied by his very lovely wife. After the luncheon they all drove in six carriages down to the *Prater* where innumerable people had assembled on foot and in carriages, to see them."

*Franz II, Roman-German Emperor. Engraving by Karl Hermann Pfeifer from an 1802 painting by Josef Hickel.*

The *Eipeldauer-Briefe* also report the *Cercle:*[34]
*Juhe! Herr Vetter! die gute Königin von Neapel ist jetzt wieder gsund! Den Sonntag ist bei Hof grosser Serkl gwesen, und der hat ein bissl glanzender augschaut als der Serkl, den mein Frau Gemahlin gibt. Da hats Brillanten gebn dass ein d'Augen weh tan haben. Der Admiral Nelson allein hat ein ganze Schatzkammer aufn Leib ghabt.*
("Hurrah! My cousin! The good Queen of Naples is now well again! On Sunday there was a great *Cercle* at Court, which was a trifle more resplendent

*81*

than the *Cercle* my wife is giving. There were such diamonds that dazzled one's eyes. Admiral Nelson alone had a whole treasury on his person").

And Count Zinzendorf makes the following note:

> *Après 11 h au Cercle pour la reine de Naples. J'y fis la connaissance de Nelson, dont la figure n'est pas si mal. La plaque Turque, l'autre plaque de l'ordre du bain, le cordon de l'ordre Napolitain de la fidélité, Me Hamilton grandondon... qui tient son chapeau ... Après le dîner Lord Minto y présente Nelson.*

("After 11 o'clock at the *Cercle* of the Queen of Naples I made the acquaintance of Nelson, whose appearance is not so bad. The Turkish Order, the Order of the Bath, the Cordon of the Neapolitan Order of Fidelity, Madame Hamilton grandondon[35] who holds his hat ... After the meal Lord Minto presented Nelson there").

On August 25th we find Nelson once again in the *Leopoldstädter Theater*, (according to Müller's journal): *Der unruhige Wanderer 2ter Theil Admiral Nelson  mit der Gfin Hamilton da gewesen.* ("The Restless Wanderer, second part, Admiral Nelson present with Lady Hamilton.")   The full title of the play was *Kasperl, der unruhige Wanderer.* ("Kasperl, the Restless Wanderer"), a dramatic fairy-tale with songs in three acts, adapted for Marinelli's stage by Hensler, with music by Wenzel Müller.   The text of this play, the first performance of which was given for the benefit of Laroche, was published in the same year.[36] The first part of the play, entitled *Der unruhige Wanderer oder Kasperles letzter  Tag* (" The Restless Wanderer or Kasperl's Last Day"), appeared for the first time in 1796.  It was fashionable at the time to write sequels to successful plays, Schikaneder treated his libretto of  Mozart's *Zauberflöte* ("Magic Flute") in this way and had the second part set to music by another composer.  He wrote as many as six sequels to his *Dummer Anton* ("Silly Anthony").

On August 27th the Court[37] moved to Baden near Vienna, a favourite summer resort of the Habsburgs, who usually occupied  the so-called *Kaiserhaus* (Emperor's House) in the main square. The Queen of Naples, who went to Baden only on September 3rd on a short visit, stayed at the Neumann house, formerly known as Gondrar house.

We must now leave this chronicle of the four friends, as we must tell of several incidents relating to Nelson which cannot be dated with accuracy.

First there is yet another proof of Nelson's popularity in Vienna.  The Department of Prints and Drawings of the British Museum preserves among its portraits of Nelson a business card from Vienna.[38] It was made for the goldsmith Karl Albrecht Böck by the engraver Bernhard Biller, probably in 1800.  Böck, who took the civic oath on June 22nd, 1798,[39] had his shop on the *Graben* in the house called *Zum grünen Kranz* (The Green Wreath), lying between the *Spiegelgasse* and the *Dorotheengasse*  on the south side. The entrance of the new building was in the *Spiegelgasse* over which was a large, golden anchor and rope. This however had nothing to do with Nelson, but with the Anchor Insurance Society, which at one time had its offices there. Böck called his shop *Zum Admiral Nelson* and his business card[40] bore a medallion picture of the Admiral.

An anecdote concerning Nelson and a wine-merchant who lived near his Inn was told to the biographer Harrison[41] by Mr. Oliver, who was engaged by our party in Vienna as interpreter: "Mr. Oliver, being one day informed that the Champagne was nearly exhausted, went immediately in search of a fresh stock. It being a prohibited article in Vienna, the merchant whom he applied to, observed that he did not sell it. Mr. Oliver then asked, where he could procure some, as he feared his lordship would have none at table. 'What!' said the merchant, 'do you want it for the great Lord Nelson?' On being answered in the affirmative he immediately replied - 'Then you shall take as much as you like; for no man on earth is more welcome to any thing I have!' Mr. Oliver took only two bottles, as the owner positively refused to receive any money from his lordship; who, with his usual benignity of heart, on being informed of this generous act immediately invited the merchant to dine with him next day." This might have been Leopold Arlet, the owner of the nearby wine vaults in the *Bognergasse*, called *Zum schwarzen Kamel* (The Black Camel), or Achatius Lenkay in the Liliengasse, the first place later frequented by Beethoven, the second by Schubert. One may conclude from a passage in Michael Kelly's "Reminiscences"[42] that it was probably the snack-bar in the *Bognergasse*, later owned by the Stiebitz family and still existing in a new building. Kelly writing of the spring of 1787, tells of a Club of noble and wine-loving Englishmen[43] in the *Graben*, and continues: "There was another place frequented by many of them after the opera was over which was neither more nor less than a grocer's shop in the same street. This grocer was supposed to have the finest champagne and hock in the country; I was his constant visitor. Behind the shop was a room, where he admitted a chosen few, but it was not open to the public. There we always found excellent Parmesan cheese, anchovies, olives and oysters. No table cloth was allowed, but each person had a large piece of brown paper presented to him by way of napkin." Kelly, who also tells us that the English introduced horse racing in the *Prater*[44] as well as lamp smashing by night in the *Graben*,[45] was not well acquainted with the local topography, and therefore it is quite likely that from memory he confused the *Bognergasse* with the *Graben* itself, especially since it is really a continuation of the same street.

Who was this Mr. Oliver, who, as we shall see, was long known to Sir William Hamilton ? There were at least two, and possibly four, men of this name living in Vienna about 1800. The first was Fr. Oliva who in 1785 translated a French play for the theatre in the *Leopoldstadt*. He is probably the same person as Franz Xaver Oliver, a clerk of the treasury, pensioned in 1793. The second was one Adam Oliver, of whom we know a little more. About 1785 he was chancery-clerk at the *K.K. Studien- und Bücherzensur- Hofkommission*

(Commission for Censorship). One of these two men, but more probably Adam Oliver, in 1791 was a member of the patriotic, counter-revolutionary "Association" - which never became effective - and edited the *Allgemeine-Bürger-Kronik* in Vienna for his friend, Leopold Alois Hoffmann. Hoffmann, a politically ambiguous writer and ex-Freemason, as official editor of the paper, received 500 florins from the Imperial private purse; but in effect Oliver did all the work.[46] Adam Oliver was born about 1753 and died on June 20th 1808 in Vienna. Another Franz Oliva, who was probably younger, was a clerk in the office of the Jewish banking firm, Offenheimer & Herz, on the *Bauernmarkt* No.620, Vienna, of which we shall hear later, and an acquaintance of Beethoven:[47] it was he who carried Beethoven's first letter to Goethe at the beginning of May 1811; during the summer of the same year he stayed with the master in Teplitz and arranged Beethoven's meeting with Varnhagen and Rachel. On June 3rd 1812 Oliva wrote to Varnhagen that he had lost his job with the banking firm and that, following Beethoven's wish, he intended to go with the master to England; the journey, as we know, was never undertaken. Oliva afterwards became bookkeeper to the wholesale firm of Joseph Biedermann, but he left Vienna in 1820 and went to Petersburg as a teacher of languages; there he married and had one daughter, Betty. He died of cholera in that city in 1848. Beethoven dedicated to him the Piano Variations in D major, op.76.2. It may have been none of these three Olivers, or Olivas, but possibly yet another, of whom Harrison writes:[48] "On the day after Nelson's arrival, the party having intended to quit Vienna almost immediately, and none of them understanding the German language, Mr. Oliver, an English linguist residing in that city, was engaged by his lordship, to act as confidential secretary and interpreter, and accompany them to England; this gentleman having been long known to Sir William Hamilton;[49] who had many years before recommended him to be employed occasionally by the King of Naples, in procuring carriages, horses, curious animals, and various other articles of pleasure and amusement, from London." Oliver is said to have remained in Nelson's service until the latter's death.

Among the new acquaintances which Nelson and the Hamiltons made in Vienna were three Jewish families, all related to each other: Arnstein, Eskeles and Herz. Here it should be mentioned, that the Empress Maria Theresa and her son Joseph II (1780-1790) had encouraged about a dozen Swiss Protestants to Vienna, who became great merchants and patrons of the arts, and who were also given titles, as for example the Count Fries. The number of Jewish bankers and wholesale merchants, who came from North Germany, however, was smaller, as tolerance towards Jews in Austria was still of very recent date. Two of these Jewish families, Arnstein and Eskeles, set up the first Jewish *Salons* in Vienna which were frequented by the best society. Nathan Adam Freiherr von Arnstein, banker, wholesale merchant and Consul General for Sweden (since 1803) lived at the *Hohe Markt*, a square north of the *Graben*. The *Hohe Markt*, more like a road than a square, was the site of the Roman military camp *Vindobona*. Arnstein's wife Franziska, called Fanny, was an ardent enemy of Napoleon.[50] Their daughter, Henrietta, married a Herr von Pereira in 1802, Nathan's sister married Salomon Herz. Bernhard von Eskeles, another banker created a baron, lived in the *Dorotheergasse*, a side street running south off the *Graben*. His wife, another sister of Fanny von Arnstein, was called Cäcilie, and they had a daughter who became a pupil of Moscheles.[51] These ladies are said to have had great charm and artistic taste. The office of Arnstein's firm[52] was in the *Bräunerstrasse*, which forks off the *Graben* between the *Habsburger-* and the *Dorotheergasse*. It is noteworthy that this firm was instrumental in obtaining English money for the relief of Tyrol during the years 1810 to 1814; from a private source £30,000 had by 1809 reached Andreas Hofer through Baring in London and the Swiss banker, Michael Steiner, in Vienna. Harrison reports:[53] "Arnstein, too, the banker, at Vienna a most opulent, liberal, munificent, and benevolent Jew, whose family may be considered as the Goldsmids[54] of Germany, gave a grand concert and splendid supper, to his Lordship and friends; at which all the foreign ministers and nobility were present."

It is doubly interesting to read what the actress Karoline Jagemann writes in her Reminiscences[55] where we learn more about Nelson's visit at the Arnsteins' which, according to her, had taken place in their country house near town.[56]

> *In ihrer sehr hübschen Behausung sah man täglich Fremde aus allen Ländern, auch Lord Nelson mit der durch ihre Attitüden bekannten Lady Hamilton wurde erwartet. Nach vielen Stunden der Ungewissheit, ob die Herrschaften der Einladung Folge leisten würden, erschienen sie endlich; Nelson, ein kleiner, magerer Mann, mit einem Auge und einem Arm, den man den Helden nicht ansah, Lady Hamilton, eine hohe, stattliche Gestalt, mit dem Kopfe einer Pallas, hinter ihm drein, seinen Hut unter dem Arme tragend. Sie blieben den ganzen Abend und liessen ihre Wirte in der grössten Satisfaktion über die ihnen gewidmete Ehre züruck.*

("In their very charming house one could daily see strangers from all countries, Lord Nelson was also expected with Lady Hamilton who had become well known through her Attitudes. After many hours of uncertainty as to whether the illustrious persons would make use of their invitation, they appeared at last; Nelson a small, thin man, with one eye and one arm, whose looks do not betray the hero, Lady Hamilton, a tall, imposing figure, with the head of a Pallas, followed him carrying his hat under her arm. They stayed all the evening and left their host filled with the greatest satisfaction for the honour shown to them").

In the late summer of 1800 Karoline Jagemann came to Vienna on a visit as actress and singer from Weimar, where she outmanoeuvred even Goethe at the Court of the Grand Duke, Karl August.[57] From August until October she appeared at the *Kärntnertor-Theater* and the *Burg-Theater*. Her first

*85*

performance was as Susanna in *Le nozze di Figaro* by Mozart (26th and 31st August) and her last as Octavia in Kotzebue's *Kleopatra* (3rd and 5th October). Strangely enough Nelson did not visit the Italian opera at the Court theatres, although he had made the acquaintance of the actress-singer. Her second visit to Vienna in 1807 was not particularly successful, but on a later occasion, in 1824, when she came solely as an actress, she achieved great success. Her description of Nelson and Lady Hamilton is of special interest, as an actress is a keener observer than the wife of an ambassador. In this connection it is noteworthy that Fräulein Jagemann, when she had become Frau von Heygendorf, had a Haydn Mass performed in her house in Weimar at the beginning of 1811, at which Goethe was present. This might have been yet another performance of the so-called Nelson Mass.

We learn from Miss Knight's autobiography[58] that Nelson and his party paid a visit to another interesting personage: "Prince Stanislaus Poniatowski, whom I had known at Rome, and who quitted that city when the French took possession of it in 1798, was then living at the Château of Lichtenstein, near Vienna, and came to see me. He invited us all to dine with him, and he received us with great cordiality, and showed us his magnificent collection of jewels, with some of the largest pearls ever seen. This prince possessed every advantage which nature and fortune could bestow. A fine person, and immense fortune, the faculty of speaking every language, and a distinguished rank in life. He declared himself an enemy to all melancholy, and yet I never saw a person whom I thought less happy. It was said that he had been disappointed with regard to the crown of Poland, a hope of obtaining which had been held out to him by the Empress Catherine". Stanislaus Poniatowski, 46 years of age at that time, was Treasurer of Lithuania, Governor of Podolia, and General in the Polish Crown Army; he was a nephew of the weak King Stanislaus II of Poland.[59] For some time he lived in Vienna, went to Rome later as a collector of works of art, and died in Florence in 1833. The "Château of Lichtenstein, near Vienna" was probably the summer palace in the suburb of Rossau. Miss Knight writes that she was present at this meeting, which she herself had effected; otherwise, as far as we know, she seldom accompanied her friends. Mrs Cadogan, it seems, was always absent; she probably was a slight embarrassment to the travelling party.

Nelson had a somewhat romantic encounter with the Hungarian Count Theodor Batthyány in Vienna. Harrison[60] gives us the following account: "An aquatic fête was also given by the Count Batthyány, on the Danube, within one mile of Vienna; where Lord Nelson was particularly invited to see some experiments made with a very large vessel, which had been projected and constructed by the Count, having machinery for working it up against the powerful stream of the rapid torrent.[61]

This vessel had been so splendidly prepared for the reception of the illustrious guests, that it would not have disgraced a congress of sovereigns.

*The Danube near Vienna, viewed from Nussdorf (engraving by C L Billwiller). This was the scene of a nautical experiment in Lord Nelson's time.*

The party were served with coffee, fruit cakes, ices, etc. in the utmost profusion, and were much pleased with their entertainment; but his lordship did not appear to consider the Count's plan, though prodigiously ingenious, as likely to answer the intended purpose. The pleasure of the day was considerably enhanced by their having previously formed a fishing party and dined on what they caught by angling, which was Sir William Hamilton's favourite diversion, at Bridgid Au, near the Au Gardens; two long-boats having convoyed the company to that charming place, with an excellent band of music." The place from which they started was probably Fischamend on the Danube below Vienna, where the Princely family of Batthyány[62] had had a country estate since 1777. The place where this water party ended, however, was Brigittenau, named after St. Bridget and situated north of the Leopoldstadt and the Danube; in olden times it was famous for its annual public festival: the Brigittenau kirmess. Brigittenau is now part of Vienna.

The first reference to the invention in question was made in 1784[63] - long before steam navigation. On October 11th of that year while on a journey to Ofen in Pressburg, Joseph II visited the ship "having machinery for working against the powerful stream of the rapid torrent", about which he made the following sceptic remark:

*Es wäre gut, wenn dieses Schiff in so viel Tagen nach Wien käme, als E.E. [Eure Exzellenz] Stunden für dessen Abreise und Ankunft ausgerechnet haben.*

("It would be well if this ship came to Vienna in as many days as Your Excellency spent hours working out its departure and arrival").[64]

Nine years later Count Theodor Batthyány is mentioned as the inventor of such a vessel. A hand written news-sheet in the Vienna *Nationalbibliothek*,[65] *Der heimliche Botschafter* (The Secret Messenger), reports on August 23rd 1793, that two such ships arrived from Pressburg at the Tabor bridge - near the Augarten in the Leopoldstadt - one for passengers, the other for freight. They were said to have been driven up-stream by means of an Archimedian screw fixed in front, and that the Count would be granted a *Privilegium exclusivum* (exclusive licence) for his invention.[66] Among the papers of Count Karl Zinzendorf,[67] there are observations of a Mr. Anton von Giuliani, about the Count's vessels on the Danube, delivered on October 18th 1793. The expert opinion bears the inscription:

*À Son Excellence Le Comte Theodore de Bathiani. Exposition d'Antoine de Giuliani sur les difficultés qu'il y a de concilier avec les principes reçus en Méchanique la Navigation nouvelle, qu'il s'agit d'entreprendre sur le Danube.*

(" To His Excellency the Count Theodore de Batthyány. Demonstration by Antoine de Giuliani, showing the difficulty involved in reconciling the known principles of mechanics with the new form of navigation which he [the Count] proposes to introduce on the Danube").

The report continues: *Alors elle pouvra comparer la force de trente ou quarante chevaux à celle qu'on éxigeroit d'une machine, par la quelle on voudroit suppléer à ce moyen.*

("Then this machine, which would replace the existing method, would be equivalent to the power of thirty or forty horses").

We find later a more detailed description of "Count Theodor Batthyány's attempt to sail up-stream on the Danube" in J.G. Megerle von Mühlfeld's *Memorabilien des Oesterreichischen Kaiserstaates* (Memoirs of the Austrian Empire):[68]

*Schon im Jahre 1793 erheilt Graf Theodor Batthyány über eine besondere und neuerfundene Bauart der Schiffe, mit welchen man auch wider den Strom fahren könne, eine Privilegium exclusivum auf 20 Jahre, unter der Signatur und Firma: Neue Königlich privilegierte Schiffsbau- und Schiffahrts-Compagnie, und zwar mit dem ausdrücklichen in dem Privilegium enthaltenen Beisatze: dass es Niemandem ohne schriftliche Erlaubnis gedachter Compagnie gestattet sein soll, sich der Bauart dieser Schiffe weder im*

*wesentlichen noch äusseren zufälligen, zu bedienen. Eben dieser*
*Graf, welcher keine andere Absicht hatte, als den Handel zu Wasser*
*zu erleichtern und hierdurch dem Staate neue Vorteile zu verschaffen,*
*erfand 1797 eine neuerliche Wasser-Maschine, womit man auf dem*
*Wasser ohne alle Menschenhände stromaufwärts fahren konnte. Er*
*machte damit am 17.September 1797 auf der Donau, an der*
*Brigittenaue, die erste Probe. Obschon diese Maschine in sich selbst*
*mehr als 700 Centner Last fasste, so wurde doch noch ein 18 Klafter*
*langer Kehlhammer mit Gedecke, nebst einer Schaluppe (zusammen*
*bei 450 Centner schwer) angeheftet. Die Maschine ging mit dieser*
*Last zur Bewunderung aller Zuschauer aufwärts ihren Weg gegen*
*den stärksten Strom des Flusses so leicht, als sie ohne diese ihr*
*beigegebene Last tat.*

("For a special and newly invented method of constructing vessels, in which one might even sail up-stream, Count Theodor Batthyány received as early as 1793 a *Privilegium exclusivum* for 20 years, under the style and title: New Royal Shipbuilding and Navigation Company, and this with the express clause contained in the *Privilegium*: that nobody should have permission, without written authority of the said company, to use the method of construction of these ships in either a substantial or superficial manner. This same Count, who had no intention other than to facilitate trade by water and thus provide new profits for the state, invented a new hydraulic engine in 1797, with which one could sail up-stream without the aid of human hands. On 17th September 1797, he tested it for the first time on the Danube, at the *Brigittenau*. Although the machine itself carried more than 700 cwt. of freight, a covered Danube freighter of 18 fathoms in length and a long boat, together weighing 450 cwt. were attached to it. To the general admiration of the onlookers, the machine with this freight went upwards on her course against the strongest current of the stream, just as easily as she did without the added freight").

This sailing test is pictured in a gouache painting by "J.A." engraved by "J.Z.", i.e. J.Zenger. The original and the engraving, the latter coloured and in black and white, are in the *Museum der Stadt Wien*. The engraving bears the inscription:

*Representatio navium novissimae inventionis Excellentissimi*
*D.comitis Theodori a Batthyán, Perpetui in Németh-Ujviir requisitis*
*desiteratae securitates, utilitatis, commoditatis, aeque ac venustatis*
*attributis gaudentium.*

("Presentation of ships, an invention of the prominent Earl Theodor von Batthyány performed on Nemeth-Ujviir for the investigation of expedients aiming the safety, utility and comfort, but also for pleasure of those enjoying them".)

The large vessel in the illustration is probably the pleasure boat, the two smaller ones are the freighters. The small vessels in the foreground are ferries;

the one at the left with the cover, is typical of Vienna at that time.
It is noteworthy that after 1790 Count Batthyány owned a factory in
Nadelburg near Wiener-Neustadt, which produced sewing needles, brass
buttons and other so-called Nuremberg products;[69] its Vienna office was in the
*Untere Bräunerstrasse*. (The *Habsburgergasse* of today was at that time called
*Obere Bräunerstrasse*). Batthyány died on June 13th 1812. His water-machine
was not a lasting success, and so Joseph II's and Nelson's doubts concerning it
were justified.

Towards the end of August, Sir Arthur Paget, Sir William Hamilton's
successor at Naples, wrote a letter to Lord Minto, which (though it takes us back
a little) is of interest to us here as an English echo from Sicily. It is dated from
Palermo, August 29th, and is printed in "The Paget Papers. Diplomatic and
other Correspondence of the Right. Hon. Sir Arthur Paget, G.C.B., 1794 - 1807.
Arranged and edited by his son, The Right-Hon. Sir August B.Paget, G.C.B.,
Late Her Majesty's Ambassador in Vienna. With notes by Mrs. J.R.Green".[70]

"I shall be curious to hear from Y$^r$ L$^p$ upon the subject of the Queen. I dread
much from the circumstances of Lady Hamilton being with Her Majesty, whose
influence is great, and whose ends are wicked ... The conduct of her Sicilian
Majesty since her departure from hence, has not given much satisfaction here,
& having dragged, as it is termed, Lady Hamilton for whom Epithets are not
spared with her to Vienna, is not considered here as very edifying for herself or
her Royal Daughters."[71]


1 Gluck's publisher and patron of Mozart.
2 *Museum der Stadt Wien*.
3 Vienna 1898/99. Vol.II. Plate 51.
4 Cf.Altmann's history of the *Bürgerspital*, Vienna 1860, p.15.
5 "Reminiscences" I, 248.
6 *Nützliches Adressen-und Reisebuch*, Vienna 1792, P310.
7 The *Zeremonial-Protokoll* in the Vienna *Haus-, Hof- und Staatsarchiv* states that on October
24th 1800 the suite of the Grand Duchess Elisabeth (the abbess, and sister of Maria Carolina)
occupied seven rooms at "Johann Willar's".
8 Pezzl's *Neue Skizze von Wien*, Part 2. p.206.
9 Copper plates, vol.II, part 2. No.68, to the text of 1819, 10th part, p.50.
10 In the 19th part, 5th letter, pp.47 et. seq.
11 Apparently Nelson occupied the best and largest room of the inn, in the centre of the first
storey.
12 III. 163 et seq.
13 cf. Pohl-Botstiber, "Haydn",III. 132 : *Als Nelson von Italien aus Eisenstadt besuchte...*
("When Nelson coming from Italy visited Eisenstadt...").
14 Part 19, 3rd letter.
15 The error originated with the Viennese bibliophile Franz Haidinger.
16 In the afternoon the temperature rose to 28.5 Deg. centigrade (appr. 96 Deg. F); this was the
maximum temperature reached during their stay (see *Wiener Zeitung*, pp.2755 and 2761).
17 "Life and Letters of ...Minto", III.146.

18 Similar reports in the *Magyar Hírmondó* on August 26th: "... where even now there are still so many people standing to see Nelson, that often he can pass only with great difficulty through the door of his lodgings, which is blocked by a crowd of onlookers."

19 Although she says, "one he took up in his arm̱s", Lady Minto does not mention why Nelson was in need of such help in society.

20 The number of boxes reserved for the Court had been increased by one since August; in the *Kärntnertor-Theater* too they were enlarged.

21 "The Dispatches and Letters of ... Nelson", IV. 265.

22 Marie Louise, later Empress of France; Ferdinand, later Emperor of Austria; Caroline, Leopoldine, Marie Clementine and Josef, the latter only a year and a half of age at the time, were the six children of Franz II.

23 See: H. Knudsen, *Reallexikon der deutschen Literaturgeschichte*, Berlin 1928, II.65.

24 Johann Nestroy's *Sämtlich Werke*, edited by F. Bruckner and O.Rommel, Vienna 1924,I.652.

25 Preserved in the *Stadtbibliothek*, Vienna.

26 Karl von Marinelli was the manager of the *Leopoldstädter Theater*.

27 Published the same year (copy in the *Nationalbibliothek*, Vienna).

28 The private introduction of the three English friends to the Emperor and the Empress took place through the Queen of Naples; they were officially presented by the British Ambassador and his wife (Harrison, "Nelson", II.250).

29 Preserved in the *Haus-, Hof- und Staatsarchiv*, Vienna.

30 Beethoven's patron.

31 Mozart took part in one of these concerts, Beethoven in others.

32 No.69, p.2753.

33 *Magyar Kurir*, No.17, p.253 et. seq. (Copy in the National Museum Budapest.)

34 No.20, 2nd letter, p.16.

35 Probably a play on words from grand-dondon and grand-cordon.

36 Copy in the *Nationalbibliothek*, Vienna.

37 The Emperor and Empress, the Crown Prince Ferdinand and the Princess Ludovica.

38 Portrait Catalogue, III.318, No.66.

39 *Archiv der Stadt Wien, Bürgerbuch, 1792-1835.*

40 The card is inscribed: *Bey Carl Albrecht Boeck, bürgerlicher Galanterie Goldarbeiter, sind alle Gattungen goldener...zu haben.* ("At Carl Albrecht Boeck's, civic Jeweller and Goldsmith, all kinds of golden [ware] ... to be had").

41 "Nelson", II.254.

42 I.260 et. seq.

43 English society in Vienna is also mentioned by Lord Craven in his "Memoirs", where he says during the first period of Sir Robert Keith's term of office as British Ambassador, about 1785, "that he had presented upwards of four hundred members of the British nobility and gentry who had come to Vienna at this period, for the court provided more gaiety, magnificence, fine music, and beautiful women than any other in Europe".

44 I.262.

45 I.271

46 Cf. *Vertrauliche Akten*, Fasc. 58, p.33 b, *Haus-, Hof- und Staatsarchiv*, Vienna.

47 Thayer-Riemann, *Beethoven*, Leipzig, 1911, Vol.III, 2nd edition, pp. 131 et. seq., etc.

48 "Nelson", II. 253 et. seq.

49 Burney, "The Present State of Music in France and Italy", second edition, London, 1773, p.324, calls Oliver "a young Englishman, who has been four years in the Conservatorio of St. Onofrio" (Naples 1770).

50 Cf. K.A.Varnhagen v. Ense, *Vermischte Schriften*, 2nd edition, Leipzig, 1843 Vol 1 pp.407 et. seq., and the earlier quotations from Mrs St. George's diary.

51 Cf. Thayer-Deiters-Riemann, *Beethoven*, Leipzig 1908, vol.V, see index.

52 Founded in 1782 by Adam Isaac Arnstein, whose grandson David was the firm's correspondent and a man of some literary ability.

53 "Nelson", II.253 et. seq.

54 Abraham Goldsmid, "helping Pitt in high finance in the Napoleonic war period and being a great friend of Nelson and Lady Hamilton, was very fond of music"; his daughter Jane had met Haydn in London (see Marion Scott, "Haydn: Relics and Reminiscences in England", "Music and Letters", London, April 1932, P.136.)

55 *Die Erinnerungen der Karoline Jagemann*, edited by Eduard von Bamberg, Dresden 1926, pp.150 et. seq.

56 It is known that the Arnstein family had a villa on the way to Schönbrunn, called *"Dreyhaus"* (The Three Houses); the Eskeles family had theirs in the suburb of Heitzing, between Schönbrunn and St. Veit.

57 She later became the mistress of the Grand Duke.

58 I. 153.

59 Another nephew of the King was Prince Joseph Anton Poniatowski (died in 1813) whom Michael Kelly ("Reminiscences", I.245) had met in Vienna through the British Ambassador, Sir Robert Keith, about 1785. Burney also met a brother of the King in Vienna in 1772 (op.cit.., I.258).

60 "Nelson", II.252 et. seq.

61 The dangerous straits of the torrent were some distance up-stream from Vienna.

62 The first owner was Prince Ludwig Batthyány. A Count Philipp Batthyány lived in Hainburg in 1800, the Austrian frontier town - further down-stream - towards Hungary, where Haydn spent his boyhood.

63 A still earlier and anonymous application for a licence to run a similar ship on the Danube was made to Maria Theresa, but this was refused by her Chancellor Kolowrat in 1778. Vide: Kurzel-Runtscheiner, *Die ersten Versuche einer Dampfschiffahrt auf der Donau 1779 - 1829* (*Jahrbuch des Vereins deutscher Ingenieure*, Vol.18 1928).

64 *Salzburger Zeitung*, 20th October 1784.

65 *Series nova*, 60,VII.137.

66 Cf. ibid., III.159 and 166 et. seq.

67 *Akten, Fasc.II, Akt f*, in the Vienna *Haus-,Hof- und Staatsarchiv*.

68 Vienna, 1825, I.57et. seq.

69 Vide: Johann Slokar, *Geschichte der österreichischen Industrie und ihre Förderung unter Kaiser Franz I*, Vienna 1914.

70 London 1896, 1. 196.

71 A satirical pamphlet was published possibly at this time in Naples, in English and Italian, describing a fête at Naples and in which the two main characters are called "Sir Sinister Teneriffe" and "Sir Pottery Lava" - the first name probably meaning Nelson and the second Hamilton. This pamphlet is mentioned in Richard Fenton's "A Tour ... through...Wales...", published anonymously (London 1811, p. 148). He mentions that the King of Naples suppressed the sale of this pamphlet in both editions, but that he (Fenton) had a copy in his collection.

# CHAPTER 9
## *An Excursion to Eisenstadt*

On September 3rd 1800, the day Queen Maria Carolina went to Baden, Haydn wrote from Eisenstadt, where he spent the summer, to his publishing firm, Artaria & Co., in Vienna:

> *Meine Fürstin, so eben von Wienn kam, sagte mir, dass die Mylady Hammelton am 6ten dieses nach Eisenstadt komen wird, allwo Sie wünschte meine Cantata Ariadne a Naxos zu singen, welche ich aber nicht besitze, bitte mir, danen hero dieselbe sobald möglich zu procuriren und anhero zu schöcken.*

("My Princess, who has just returned from Vienna, told me that Mylady Hamilton will come to Eisenstadt on the 6th inst. where she wishes to sing my Cantata Ariadne a Naxos, which however I do not possess and therefore would

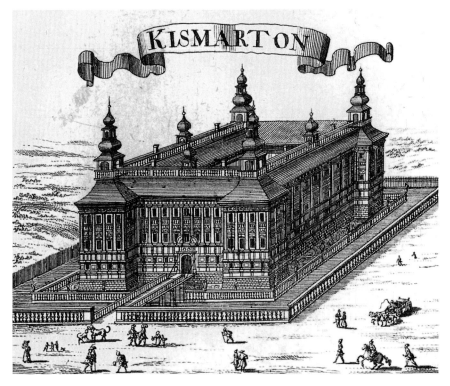

*The Esterházy Castle at Eisenstadt, which in Haydn's time was in Hungary and was known as Kismarton.*

93

ask you to procure and send here as soon as possible.[1]")

From this we can see that Princess Esterházy and Lady Hamilton first met in Vienna, where it is also likely that the Prince met Nelson . The Esterházy town palace in the *Wallnergasse* (the only side street off the *Kohlmarkt*) was very close to the inn where our party lodged.  The Cantata *Arianna a Naxos*, which Lady Hamilton probably performed with Haydn at the piano, was first sung by Signora Pacchierotti, also accompanied by Haydn, on February 18th 1791, at a public performance in London, where it  became a popular concert piece.[2] It was first published in Vienna by Artaria in 1790 and then in London by the composer in 1791.

On September 4th, before the visit to Eisenstadt, a dinner was arranged for Nelson  by the Duke Albrecht of Saxony-Teschen.  Count Zinzendorf notes in his diary:

Diné chez le duc Albert a 26 pers[onnes]  2 Hamiltons, l'amiral Nelson.

(" Dined at Duke Albert's with 26 persons present.  2 Hamiltons, the Admiral Nelson.")

Other guests at the banquet included Princess Kaunitz, the widow of the Chancellor, the Princes Dietrichstein[3] and Lobkowitz,[4] Count Lamberg (see later) as well as other members of the high aristocracy.  The reception took place in the Duke's new palace, which stood on the *Augustinerbastei* near the *Kärntnertor* and which today still houses his world famous prints and drawings the "Albertina" collection.

It seems that on September 5th, the day Malta capitulated, the Emperor and the Empress returned to Vienna from Baden.  On September 6th, when the Emperor left to  join the Army in Tyrol[5] with his young brother Archduke Johann, Lord Nelson wrote to Lord Minto:[6]

"September 6th,1800. My dear Lord, - Many thanks for your kind note; and we must all approve of the conduct of Captain Ricketts:[7] it will teach the Cisalpines that it is dangerous to touch edged tools.  We have seen the Queen this morning.  The Emperor left town at six o'clock; the Empress very melancholy but the Queen, I think, reconciled to the propriety of the Emperor's going to the Army: but it will be very difficult to make her, in any degree bear Thugut.  She thinks he will in the end deceive us. I hope it is true that our troops are landed in Holland:  it must create a powerful diversion in favour of the Austrian army.  I long for a battle, and the sooner after the Armistice the better.  We are all well, and wish for your company, and beg our best regards to Lady Minto, and all your family.  Believe me for ever, your truly obliged and affectionate, - Bronte Nelson of the Nile."

On the same day James Harris, eldest son of the first Earl of  Malmesbury and Viscount Fitzharris, wrote to his father:[8]

" St.Veit, September 6th,1800 ... The Emperor set off for the army on the Inn to-day; a fine spirited conduct, certainly the wisest and best to be pursued at such a conjuncture.  Lord Nelson and the Hamiltons dined here the other day; it is really disgusting to see her with him, but he personally is not changed: open and honest, not the least vanity about him; he gave us a short account of the Battle of Aboukir ... He looks very well but seems to be in no hurry to sail again".[9]   The young Lord, who was just starting his diplomatic career,[10] although he was more interested in literature and sport than diplomacy, lived in Vienna with his uncle and aunts and went with their eldest son Gilbert, the second Earl of Minto, to Eisenstadt on the 6th.

Lady Minto wrote to Lady Malmesbury[11] on the following day: "Vienna September 7. - You will all be in great surprise in England to hear that the Emperor is going to take command of his army himself as the best measure for doing away with party spirit and evil dispositions ... I told Nelson I wished he had the command of the Emperor's army. He said, 'I'll tell you what. If I had, I would only use one word - advance, and never say retreat.'"

On Saturday September 6th, Nelson and the Hamiltons went to visit Prince Esterházy in Eisenstadt, where, as we know, Lord Minto stayed in the previous year and where the Queen of Naples had every intention of going at the end of the year. The magnificent castle is about 40 miles south east of Vienna.

There are a few eyewitness accounts of this visit of our party to Hungary, the most important being another letter of young Lord Malmesbury to his father- "St.Veit,

September 10,1800. -  I am just returned with Gilbert from a chasse of Prince Esterházy's, and found a servant going to England. We have been there three or four days, and were received in the kindest and most hospitable manner possible.  On Sunday we had in the evening a grand firework.  On Monday, which was her Jour de fête, there was a very good ball, and yesterday the chasse. Nelson and the Hamiltons were there; we never sat down to dinner or supper less than sixty or seventy persons, in a fine hall, superbly illuminated; in short the whole in a most princely style.  Nelson's health was drunk with a flourish of trumpets and firing of cannon.  Lady Hamilton is without exception the most coarse, ill-mannered, disagreeable woman I ever met with.  The Princess with great kindness had got a number of musicians, and the famous Haydn, who is in their service, to play, knowing Lady Hamilton was fond of music.  Instead of attending to them she sat down to the Faro tables and played Nelson's cards for him, and won between 300 L. and  400 L.[12]  He told me he had no thoughts of serving again,[13] in short I could not disguise my feeling, and joined in the general abuse of her. The following is the list of what was killed (at the chasse) and in three hours, for the rain obliged us to leave off an hour and a half sooner than was intended: 63 hares, 3 pheasants, 622 partridges, 25 quails; total 703[actually 713]."

Reviewing the entertainment provided by the Esterházy's for their guests: on Sunday evening there was the firework display in the great park of the castle; the 8th - the Roman Catholic festival of the Birth of the Virgin Mary was celebrated by a special Mass in the chapel or in the *Bergkirche*, followed in the

*Nikolaus Count Esterhazy II, fourth in his family to engage Haydn as Kapellmeister. Engraving by Joseph Neidl.*

evening by the ball in the spendid *Sala terrena*, and on Tuesday there was the "chasse". On the 7th, and perhaps also on the 9th, there was probably serious music in the evenings. In all, four concerts are said to have taken place, of which two were arranged and directed by Haydn himself.

The young Lord's criticism of Lady Hamilton was harsh as was that of his aunt. She had written to her sister, Lady Malmesbury, on July 6th:[14] "Nelson and the Hamiltons all lived together in a house [at Naples] of which he bore the expense, which was enormous, and where every sort of gaming went on half the night. Nelson used to sit with large parcels of gold before him and generally go to sleep, Lady Hamilton taking from the heap without counting, and playing with his money to the amount of 500 L. a night. Her rage is play, and Sir

*Another engraving by the well-known Viennese engraver Neidl depicts Haydn, after a miniature painting by Johann Zitterer of about 1795.*

William says when he is dead, she will be a beggar". Lady Minto received this information from one Mr. Rushout who had been in Naples.[15] Her nephew was even less just, for he does not mention the musical events, in which Lady Hamilton took part. All the more reason why we should quote a letter of Griesinger, the Haydn biographer, to the Leipzig publishing firm Breitkopf & Härtel, dated Vienna, the 21st January 1801:[16]

> *An Mylady Hamilton fand Haydn einen grossen Verehrer. Sie machte einen Besuch auf Esterházys Gütern in Ungarn, bekümmerte sich aber wenig um seine Herrlichkeiten, und wich zwei Tage hindurch nie von Haydns Seite.*

("In Mylady Hamilton, Haydn found a great admirer. She paid a visit to Esterházy's estates in Hungary but was little concerned with its splendours, and for two days she never left Haydn's side").

This, too, was the impression created by Lady Hamilton on the master himself. It is unlikely in the narrow confines of the castle that there were any card games during a concert under Haydn's direction[17] - either in the same or in an adjoining room, (as was often the case in the Court Opera Houses of Europe in those days). Moreover Haydn gave Lady Hamilton a special token of his esteem on the last day of her visit, to Eisenstadt. In the collection of W.H. Cummings, sold by auction at Sotheby's on May 17th 1917, was the copy of Haydn's song: "The Spirit's Song" (Anne Hunter), copied by Elssler, with a note in Emma's handwriting: "Given to me by the admirable Haydn, in Eisenstadt. November 1800".[18]

For a better understanding of the reports on these three days, it should be mentioned, that the Esterházy Princes were the richest among the hospitable Hungarian nobles, who owned many castles, including Esterház and Eisenstadt. They had their own castle theatre and of course their own orchestra;[19] they even had their own militia, not to mention hunting and fishing grounds, stables, vineyards, cattle and farms. It was an entire state within a state. The music treasures, the numerous valuable string instruments, the manuscripts and printed music of great value, including many of Haydn's autographs are, it is true, no longer in Eisenstadt, but in Budapest. The luxury in the castle and the scale of hospitality accorded to Nelson and his party is confirmed by Harrison's description:[20] "Here they were entertained, for four days, with the most magnificent and even sovereign state. A hundred grenadiers none of them under six feet in height, constantly waited at table where every delicacy was sumptuously served up in profusion."

The reporter of the Hungarian newspaper *Magyar Hírmondó* (September 12th) writes on September 9th from Ödenburg (Sopron) which was in the same *Comitat* (Hungarian county) as Eisenstadt:[21]

"I was myself in Eisenstadt and rejoiced at the sight of Nelson , the hero of the sea. As for his figure, he is not a tall man and looks rather haggard.[22] In his small round face I would probably not have recognised his great talent, if it were not already known to me by what is now common knowledge and through the conversation of the English people in his company. He is only 41 years of age. He talks very little, especially when he is among his friends. He speaks the language of England, understanding, however, some French and Italian. I talked to him in these two languages. He praised the charming landscape of our homeland. Then I mentioned that a number of learned inhabitants of this same country made fine Latin verses in his praise when two years ago he smashed the French fleet in Aboukir.[23] At this he showed his joy and gratitude, in looks and words. I saw the result of the blow he received on his forehead in this battle, a scar in the shape of a crescent over his right eye. One of his eyes is weak; it was injured at Calvi, a port of the Isle of Corsica and therefore he needed to study a map of the Hungarian counties which our gentry had published. His right arm,

*The Bergkirche (hill church) in Eisenstadt (17th century engraving). This church, with its bizarre Calvary hill, was the performance venue for most of Haydn's late masses, possibly including one performed in Nelson's presence. Today it contains Haydn's mausoleum.*

hit between shoulder and elbow, was blown off about four years ago by a cannonball before Teneriffe, an island of the Canaries in the Atlantic Ocean. Depending on his left hand, he already writes entire letters with it. He wears a blue uniform, the empty right sleeve of which is fastened to the breast. On his left side are three shining stars: the uppermost came from the Emperor of the Turks who had it made for him after the battle of Aboukir, in the shape of a crescent; the second came from the King of Naples, whereas the third was sent by the English King, as far as I know, on the occasion of the same victory. In addition to these three orders, there are three golden commemoration medals on Nelson's breast, which he won by other deeds.[24] He carries with him fabulous treasures and apart from these his yearly income is 20,000 gold pieces... Nelson came to Eisenstadt with Sir William Hamilton who resided for forty years in Naples as English Ambassador. Hamilton is more than 70 years of age. He married his present wife in Naples[actually in London]. Lady Hamilton is a 35-year-old, tall, Englishwoman with a very handsome face, who knows well how to conduct herself. One of her many rare qualities is her clear, strong voice, with which, accompanied by the famous Haydn, she filled the audience with

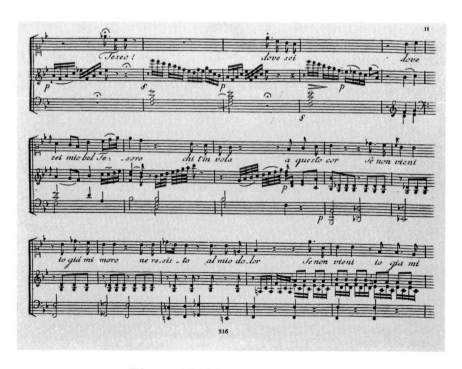

*Title page of Haydn's cantata Arianna a Naxos*

such enthusiasm that they almost became ecstatic.[25] Many were reminded of the pictures of the goddesses Dido and Calypso, and the stories of Aeneas and Telemachas. The Lady made a great name for herself with her tableaux vivants, which she has brought to the greatest perfection, especially the single postures and those arranged in company, the so-called 'Attitudes' and 'Groups'. One cannot watch them without great emotion. Drawings were made of many of her enchanting postures and movements, which were shown to the world in the form of engravings.[26] The grey haired Lord himself is well versed in matters of learning. He repeatedly climbed the volcanic Mount Vesuvius, and this under no small danger, and published his studies in a work adorned with rich illustrations.[27] It is unlikely that any Prince of Europe, let alone a private collector, has a similar collection of so-called Etrurian-Etruscan vases.

He has already published reproductions of those vases in four large folio volumes.[28] He sent his entire collection of the rarest objects to England."[29]

Nothing certain is known about the musical events during those days in Eisenstadt. It can be presumed that Lady Hamilton sang the Cantata *Arianna a Naxos*, accompanied on the piano by Haydn. It is possible that the three Anglican guests were present at the Roman Catholic High Mass on the morning of 8th September, either in the chapel of the castle or in the *Bergkirche*, and that Haydn's Mass of 1798 was again performed.[30] Harrison suggests, as we shall see, that the "Creation" was performed at Eisenstadt. The Nelson Aria by Haydn, which will be mentioned in greater detail later, was, as far as we know, requested by Lady Hamilton; there is no suggestion of its performance at Eisenstadt.

On the day of the English visitors' arrival at Eisenstadt, the 6th of September, Haydn wrote another letter from there to his publishers in Vienna.[31] He asks them to send a copy of his "Creation" to "Mr. Charles Silvester, Messenger, at Lord Grinvill's office, London". In the list of subscribers the name is spelt "Sylvester". "Lord Grinvill" is probably William Wyndham Baron Grenville, Foreign Secretary from 1791 until 1801. Since the subscribers' list contains various English names,[32] there is no reason to suppose that Mr. Sylvester's subscription was arranged by one of the English visitors to Eisenstadt on the first day of their arrival.

1 The original is in private possession.
2 It is in fact an Aria for Alto voice, which Nancy Storace sang in 1791 on the occasion when Haydn received his Honorary degree at Oxford.
3 There were two Counts Dietrichstein connected with Naples: Karl Johann Walter Count Dietrichstein, the Master of the Horse, was in Naples during 1786/7, where he was Emma's *cavaliere servante*; she used to call him "Draydixton". Moritz Count Dietrichstein, later the *Hofmusikgraf*, had been Mack's Adjutant from 1798.
4 Probably Franz Joseph Alex Prince Lobkovitz, Beethoven's friend.

5 Six days later already the Emperor came back, disappointed and disappointing.

6 "The Dispatches and Letters of...Nelson", IV.266.

7 Sir Nicholas Harris Nicolas, the editor of Nelson's letters, adds to this: "Captain William Ricketts of the El Corso Sloop, with the Pigmy Cutter, was sent by Lord Keith to destroy some vessels in the Port of Cesenatico on the 26th of August, which was fully accomplished by their boats, under Lieutenant James Lucas Yeo."

8 "Series of Letters of the First Earl of Malmesbury, his Family and Friends, from 1745 to 1820. Edited with Notes &c., by his Grandson, the Right. Hon. third Earl of Malmesbury, G.C.B.2, London 1870, II.22 et. seq. This as well as the following letter have wrongly been placed with the correspondence for 1806 by the editor of the book (II. 23, et. seq.), and that is why the writer of the letters is already called Lord Fitzharris. His father got his secondary title on December 29th 1800. In Walter Sichel's "Emma Lady Hamilton", 3rd Edition, London 1907, p.332/3t, the letter is erroneously quoted as being on p.222; Sichel also believed, that the scene took place at Esterházy in St.Veit, which led to a further misunderstanding in Pohl-Botstiber's "Haydn" (III-164).

9 Two months later, Sir Thomas Troubridge, who returned to England before Nelson, wrote to a young Lieutenant who wanted to sail on the next ship to be commanded by the hero: "I do not think he will serve again." (A.T.Mahan, "The Life of Nelson", 2nd Edition, London 1899, p.440).

10 He later became Governor of the Isle of Wight.

11 "Life and Letters of ... Minto", III-150.

12 Sichel adds: "Haydn, it must be thought, was hardly a suitable accompaniment to cards".

13 Cf. Sir Thomas Troubridge's letter, quoted above.

14 "Life and Letters of ...Earl of Minto", III. 139.

15 About Nelson and Lady Hamilton at the gambling tables, cf. Michel Palmieri de Micciché, *Moeurs de la Cour et des Peuples de Deux Siciles*, Paris 1837, pp.40-42.

16 Pohl-Botstiber, "Haydn", III.165.

17 Haydn himself would not have been expected to direct "table" or "conversation" music.

18 Now in private possession (Editorial Note).

19 The opera, however was closed with the death of Prince Nikolaus I in 1790, the orchestra was broken up, respectively drastically reduced.

20 "Nelson", II.252.

21 The German *Pressburger Zeitung* on September 16th, had a notice about the trip of the three English friends from Vienna to Eisenstadt (erroneously dating it September 8th).

22 Nelson was similarly described, on August 26th, in the *Magyar Kurir*, which called him "a profound philosopher".

23 This is a rather exaggerated allusion to Hödl's Nelson hymn (p.82).

24 Probably the two large gold medals awarded to flag officers by the Admiralty after the battles of St.Vincent and the Nile. The orders were the Turkish "Crescent", the Neapolitan "St.Ferdinand" and the English "Bath".

25 Probably the Cantata *Arianna a Naxos*.

26 Friedrich Rehberg's album of drawings made in Naples, published as engravings by Thomas Piroli (Rome) and dedicated to Sir William Hamilton. Anonymous caricatures were made from this album in London in 1807, after Nelson's death. The original was reviewed by one H. T., who enjoyed Emma's hospitality in Naples, in Wieland's *Teutscher Merkur* (Weimar) in 1794.

27 Following the publication of "Observations on Mount Vesuvius, Mount Etna and other volcanoes", :London 1772, there appeared: "Campi Phlegraei. Observations on the Volcanoes of the two Sicilies as they have been communicated to the Royal Society of London". English and French, With Supplement, Folio, Naples 1776-79. The German edition of the *Beobachtungen* (Observations) was published in Berlin in 1773. "An Account of the Earthquakes in Calabria, Sicily etc." was published in 1783.

28 *Antiquités Etrusques, Greques et Romaines, tirées du cabinet de M. Hamilton par P.F. Hugues, dit d'Hancarville*, English and French, 4 vols, Naples 1766-67. The *Recueil de Gravures d'après de Vases antiques*, was published, as stated, in Naples in 1791-1795, with outline drawings by the painter H. Morghen Tischbein. Hamilton was patron of the engraver, and adviser to Lord Elgin, and it was he who caused the Court of Naples to take an interest in Pompeii and who aided Piaggi in Herculaneum. His "Account of the Discoveries at Pompeii" was published in London in 1777.

29 This report was quoted before by Andre Csatkai in *Sopronvármegye* on 25th October 1923. Cf. the *Ödenburger Zeitung* of October 14th 1926.

30 Recently there are indications, that even Haydn's Grand Tedeum of the later period might have been performed the first time at this occasion, or on the Immaculate Conception, Monday 8th September 1800 (Editorial remark).

31 Franz Artaria and Hugo Botstiber, *Joseph Haydn und das Verlagshaus Artaria*, Vienna 1909, pp.82 et.seq.

32 Among them ten members of the Royal Family, and Lady Malmesbury.

# CHAPTER 10
## *Back in Vienna*

According to Harrison the three illustrious visitors were four days away from Vienna and therefore arrived in the capital, together with the two young English gentlemen, at noon on Wednesday, the 10th of September. On the evening of their return, we find Nelson and Emma without Sir William - again visiting the *Leopoldstädter Theater*. Müller notes in his journal in the usual form: *Die Teufelsmühle oper. 49 mal. Admiral Nelson und Gfin Hamilton da gewesen.*

("'The Devil's Mill' opera. For the 49th time. Admiral Nelson and Lady Hamilton were present"). This play, *Die Teufelsmühle am Wienerberg*, an Austrian fairy play with songs, in four acts, "based on an ancient saga", by Leopold Huber, arranged by Hensler for Marinelli's stage, with music by Müller, was performed here from 1799 until 1860.[1]

There was rain and a storm over Vienna on September 11th, and the spreading epidemic of small-pox made the times unpleasant. However, on Monday, the 15th, we find the inseparable pair back at the *Kasperltheater*: "*Kaspars Schelmereien. Admiral und Gfin Hamilton da gewesen*" (" 'Kaspar's Rogueries.' Admiral and Lady Hamilton were present") notes the accurate Müller. The sub-title of this anonymous show was: ... *oder Die Frauenzimmer-Hofmeisterin, Madame Quelque chose, ein auf die Person des Kaspars gut eingerichtetes Lustspiel, wozu Les Fourberies de Scapin nach Molièren und ein wälsches Stück dieses Titels Anlass gegeben haben.* ("...or The Ladies' Governess, Madame Quelque chose, a comedy well suited to Kaspar's character, which was based on "Les Fourberies de Scapin" by Molière and an Italian play with the same title.") This play was never printed but had formed part of the repertoire of this stage since 1781.

On September 16th or 18th - the later date was fixed as an alternative in case of bad weather- the last firework display of the year took place in the *Prater.* This display was arranged by Kaspar Stuwer, the son the master of fireworks mentioned earlier for his Nelson display of 1798. Whether Nelson was among the audience or not it is impossible to say.

Maria Carolina, who was living in Schönbrunn, and who came to the *Hofburg* only by chance, appears to have written the following undated letter to Lady Hamilton on Tuesday, September 16th:[2]

"My dear dear Lady, ever shall I be the same to you. I shall go tomorrow into the city for you about three o'clock. If you will come to my apartments we shall be alone. If that time should be inconvenient to you, come on Thursday morning to Schönbrunn, on Wednesday for the day. I shall have so much to say to you, and to our friend Nelson. I see clouds lowering and fear approaching events. I am prepared for all. On Saturday I go to Baden, and hoped to have seen you there, but your letter disappoints me. Your departure afflicts me. It is not easy to replace such friends as you; but I must hope to see you again at Naples[3] Adieu. Your sincere and grateful friend till death - a thousand compliments to the Chevalier, and to the hero - to you every thing." The Queen visited Lady Minto on September 17th and on the 18th Lady Hamilton with Nelson appears to have been with the Queen in Schönbrunn. It seems that Maria Carolina had abandoned the second expedition to Baden.

On September 19th Lady Minto wrote to Lady Malmesbury:[4] "I had a visit the day before yesterday from the Queen of Naples and her three daughters. She knows this place very well, as it was her mother's".

There is another letter of Nelson's written to Lord Minto on the 19th:[5] "Friday Morning.- My dear Lord,- We cannot dine with you to-day; but will, with much pleasure, on Saturday, the day before our departure. I wish, my dear friend, you would visit the neglected Queen of Naples: she will be glad to see and talk with you. She is scarcely ever out in the afternoon between five and six. Our best compliments to all in your house. Believe me ever, yours, - Bronte Nelson of the Nile." To which is added a postscript by Lady Hamilton: "Do, my dear Lord, go to the Queen. She told me yesterday she would be glad to see you. You need not send - go to her apartment. - E.H."

On the next day Nelson wrote to his wife:[6] "Vienna Sept 20th 1800. - My -Dear Fanny, - Since I wrote to you from Trieste, we have been so continually prepared to set out that I have not wrote a line till this day. Sir William Hamilton being recovered we set out tomorrow and shall be in England the 2nd week in October. I have wrote to Davison[7] to take a house or good lodging for the very short time I shall be in London, to which I shall instantly proceed and hope to meet you in the house. You must expect to find me a worn out old man. Make my kindest love to my Father whom I shall see the moment I have been with the King. May God bless you and believe me your affectionate - Bronte Nelson of the Nile."

The departure of the party was thus already planned for Sunday, September 21st, but in spite of the political unrest prevailing at that time, it was postponed for a few days at the request of the Queen of Naples. Apparently the departure of the party was planned now for the night of September 23rd. The following events which we shall describe account more reasonably for this second postponement. On the 22nd Haydn returned to Vienna from his summer holidays at Eisenstadt, and round about the 25th the Emperor was expected back at the residence, since Austria had arranged another 45-day truce with France.

On the evening of September 22nd, Nelson and Lady Hamilton were once more at the *Leopoldstädter Theater*. *"Raul Créqui oper. Admiral Nelson und Gfin Hamilton da gewesen.":* ("Raoul de Créqui, opera. Admiral Nelson and Lady Hamilton were present"), Wenzel Müller notes for the last time in his theatre diary. *Raoul, Herr von Créqui, oder: Die verhinderte Grausamkeit*

(Raoul Sir de Créqui, or: Cruelty Prevented), an operetta in three acts after J. M. Boutet de Monvel by Joachim Perinet[8], with music by Nicholas Dalayrac, was performed here for the first time in 1793 for the benefit of Anton Baumann.[9]

On the following day, September 23rd, the Queen of Naples wrote this letter to Lady Hamilton:[10]

> *23 Settembre 1800. Ma chere Miledy et tendre amie j'ai ete touche aux larmes de notre separation et de votre attachement dont vous m'avez donne tant de preuves et les plus recentes ce matin que le ciel vous benisse et rend heureuse comme mon coeur vous le souhaite et que je puisse avoir bientot la consolation de vous revoir a Naples je vous repete ce que vous ai toujours dit dans tous le temps circostances endroits Emme la chere Emme sera mon ami soeur et ce sentiment sera toujours le meme comptez la dessus recevez de nouveau mes remerciments pour tous ce que vous avez fait et pour l'amitie sincere que vous m'avez temoigne ecrivez moi donez moi vos nouvelles je vous ferois parvenir le mienes menagez votre sante mes complimens assurances d'amitie et reconnaissance du Chevalier milles et milles remercimens au heros Nelson dont la memoire est emprunte en terme inefacable dans mon coeur reconnaissant Adieu puisse le Ciel vous accorder ce que vous desire et souhaite le coeur attache devoue de votre tendre mere et amie - Charlotte.*
>
> *Voyez la lettre pour la reine et l'honete Castelcigala par un Courier a nous je vous enverrois pour Circello alle Castelcigalo et Miledy Spencer en Angleterre des lettres saluez tout le monde et croyez moi toute a vous reconnaissante et que vous me retrouverez votre amie toujours le meme Adieu.*

(" September 23, 1800.- My dear Lady and tender Friend, I was affected to tears at our separation, and your attachment, of which you have given me so many proofs even to the last moment. That heaven may bless and make you happy is the wish of my heart. May I soon have the consolation of seeing you again at Naples. I repeat what I have already said, that at all times and places, and under all circumstances, Emma, dear Emma, shall be my friend and sister, and this sentiment will remain unchanged. Receive my thanks once more for all you have done, and for the sincere friendship you have shown me - let me hear from you, I will manage to let you hear from me. Take care of your health. My compliments and assurances of friendship and gratitude to the Chevalier, a thousand thousand thanks to the hero Nelson, the recollection of whom my heart will ever retain. Adieu! that heaven may accord you all you desire is the heartful wish of your devoted and attached mother and friend, Charlotte. Enclosed is the letter for the Queen[11] and the honest Castelcicala.[12] By one of our couriers I will send you letters, or Circello[13] at Castelcicala, and Lady Spencer[14] in England, and believe me your grateful and ever sincere friend. Adieu!"

We shall come back later to the actual parting of the three friends from the Queen.

On September 22nd, Haydn brought back a new work which although short, is of great concern to us in this story. The *Magyar Hírmondó* of September 23rd reported:

" Lady Hamilton had asked Herr Joseph Haydn, the most praiseworthy and famous conductor of Prince Esterházy, to set to music certain English verses. The subject of these verses being the heroic deeds of Admiral Nelson. Yesterday Herr Haydn returned from Hungary:  with his grand music completed, to the great joy of all those concerned.  Tonight Lord Nelson, Sir Hamilton and his wife intend to leave for Hamburg where they will board a ship for England".

While she was in Naples, in September 1798, Miss Knight had written a hymn on Nelson's victory at Aboukir, which Lady Hamilton sent to Lady Nelson in London in September 1798,[15] but it was still unprinted in 1800, and it may be that the nickname "Nelson's charming poet laureate", which the English navy had given her, deterred the poetess from printing the poem at Naples; or perhaps she considered the fact that many other poems on Nelson had already been published in Italy; for instance there appeared at Naples:

> *Il felice arrivo nella Citta di Napoli del Gran Ammiraglio di  S.M.*
> *Brittanica Orazio Nelson dopo la celebre vittoria riportata sopra la*
> *Flotta Francese nelle Bocche de Nilo, il giorno 1. Agosto 1798.*
> *Cantata a voce sola con cori, musica del Signor D. Giuseppe*
> *Gargano. Napoli presso Vincenzio Orsino regio tipografo. 1798.*

("Horatio Nelson's the Great Admiral of His Britannic Majesty, fortunate arrival at the city of Naples after the famous victory  over the French Fleet at the mouth of the Nile on August 1st, 1798.  Cantata for solo voice and chorus, composed by Signor Giuseppe Gargano.  Naples, printed by Vincenzio Orsino, Royal typographer 1798").[16]

Another poem appeared in Pisa: "On Lord Nelson's Victory over the French Fleet at Abouquir.  An idyl by P.P.D.D. Pisa, From the New Typographical Press. MDCCXCVIII"[17].

Let us now hear what Miss Knight has to say about those days in Austria and about her poem:[18] "Great curiosity was expressed to behold the hero of the Nile at every place on the road to Vienna.  I cannot say that I enjoyed the journey, for I was dreadfully fatigued, far from well, and uneasy on many accounts, besides being a good deal injured by the carriage being overturned in which I was travelling.  At Vienna, whenever Nelson appeared in public, a crowd was collected, and his portrait was hung up over many shops - even the milliners giving his name to particular dresses - but it did not appear to me that the English nation was at all popular.  The people generally were opposed to the war with France, which had proved so unfavourable to them, for, although the troops were brave and loyal, they were not well  commanded.  We often had music, as the best composers and performers were happy to be introduced to Sir William and Lady Hamilton. I was much pleased with Haydn. He dined with us, and his conversation was modest and sensible. He set to music some English verses, and, amongst others, part of an ode I had composed after the battle of the Nile, and which was descriptive of the blowing up of *L'Orient:*[19]

> Britannia's leader gives the dread command;
> Obedient to his summons flames arise:
> The fierce explosion rends the skies.
> And high in air the pond'rous mass is thrown
> The dire concussion shakes the land.
> Earth, air, and sea united groan.
> The solid Pyramids confess the shock,
> And their firm bases to the centre rock.

Haydn accompanied Lady Hamilton on the piano when she sang this piece, and the effect was grand. He was staying at that time with Prince Esterházy, and presided over the famous concerts given by that nobleman at his magnificent palace in Hungary." (Then follows the well known story of Haydn's "Farewell Symphony").

The two reports of the origin and first performance of Haydn's Nelson aria, that is to say, the topical notice in the *Magyar Hírmondó* and the later memories of Miss Knight, can only be explained thus: Lady Hamilton gave the text to Haydn at Eisenstadt, where he set it to music - after the visit of the English party - in the middle of September; later he brought the composition back to Vienna where he accompanied Lady Hamilton on the piano when she sang the aria for the first time. We suggest this took place at Haydn's house, or at the inn on the *Graben* or at Prince Esterházy's nearby town-palace - in any case it was not at Eisenstadt.

The complete text by Miss Knight and Haydn's aria were until recently unknown, or more correctly, forgotten. Carl Ferdinand Pohl, the great Haydn biographer, copied the manuscript of the aria for his own use in 1868, when he was working on the Haydn music in the Esterházy archives; his successor, Hugo Botstiber, who contined Pohl's work, had this copy in his keeping when finishing the third volume of the Haydn biography. When the present author began his research on Nelson's stay in Vienna in the autumn of 1929 - see preface - his interest was aroused by Pohl's copy of the aria and he at once searched for a copy of the complete poem by Miss Knight. The poem, produced in the form of a booklet of 14 pages, was privately printed in Vienna in 1800. The author was fortunate enough to find the only two copies known to exist. One is the copy which Nelson himself presented to the Vienna *Hofbibliothek* (now the *Nationalbibliothek*) in September 1800; the other was given by Nelson about the same time to a private individual in Vienna, and later was bought by

# THE

# BATTLE OF THE NILE.

*A PINDARICK ODE.*

TO HIS EXCELLENCY

THE Rt. HONBLE.

## SIR WILLIAM HAMILTON,

K. B. HIS BRITANNICK MAJESTY'S

MINISTER PLENIPOTENTIARY AND ENVOY EXTRAORDINARY

AT THE COURT OF THE TWO SICILIES

ETC. ETC. ETC.

*VIENNA,*

PRINTED BY WIDOW ALBERTI.

1800.

*A poem by Miss Cornelia Knight about the Battle of the Nile was published in English in Vienna. Haydn was invited to set it to music. In fact he composed an aria for soprano with piano accompaniment for ten of the seventeen verses of the poem. Nelson presented the Vienna Hofbibliothek with an autographed copy of this edition.*

*109*

*Before his departure Nelson sat for the well known Viennese painter Heinrich Füger, and it is to him that we owe one of the finest portraits of the naval hero.*

the Vienna University Library through the antiquarian book trade. There is no evidence to show that any of the four English friends took a copy of the poem to their home country or that they took steps to have one preserved in England. Even Miss Knight in her autobiography does not quote the poem from print, and the "Nelson Papers" in the British Museum, which among many important documents also contain numerous poems (even from current journals), do not include this Vienna print. The booklet was printed by a good firm, the founder of which - Ignaz Alberti - was also a Freemason.[20]

The cost of this edition was perhaps borne by Maria Carolina but it can only have been a small one.[21] The title-page reads: "The Battle of the Nile. A Pindarick Ode. To his Excellency The Rt. Honble. Sir William Hamilton, K.B. His Britannick Majesty's Minister Plenipotentiary and Envoy Extraordinary At the Court of the Two Sicilies etc.etc.etc. Vienna, printed by Widow Alberti. 1800.[22]" On pages 3 and 4 is the Preface by the authoress dated: Naples, 15th September 1798, that is to say six weeks after the battle, and signed, so that the anonymity of the title is immediately cancelled. From this preface we learn that Sir William himself had inspired the poem; here too Cornelia mentions her late father.

The copy in the *Nationalbibliothek* bears Nelson's inscription (written with his left hand and marred by two ink-spots): "From Bronte Nelson of the Nile, presented to His Imperial Majesty's Library at Vienna in September 1800". Thus Nelson obviously intended it for the public *Hofbibliothek*, and not for the

Emperor's private library (the so-called *Fideikomissbibliothek*, which is now part of the *Nationalbibliothek*). The other copy which the *Universitätsbibliothek* bought for 10 Kreuzer (about twopence) from the second-hand bookshop of Gilhofer & Ranschburg in Vienna in 1888, bears on page 2 the following dedication[23] "Presented to Mr. van Schorel on the 5th September 1800 By Bronte Nelson of the Nile at Vienna." From this it is clear that the poem was already printed at the end of August and was available when the party went to Eisenstadt on September 6th; this made it possible for Lady Hamilton to have given Haydn a printed copy during their visit. No copy, however, was found among Haydn's belongings. Nelson certainly gave copies of the poem to other people in Vienna. The only private person whose copy we know to have been preserved is Schorel, a Belgian of whose connection with Nelson nothing is known. Peter Johann Franz d'Egmont van Schorel, Seignor de Wilryck, was born in Antwerp in 1748 and became Lord Mayor of that City in 1788/9. In 1800 he was obviously a private person and lived at No.39 in Obermeidling, a suburb of Vienna. He died a widower in Vienna on April 25th, 1805 at the *Kohlmarkt* No.300. Later we shall have something to say about his younger brother, Charles, in Prague.

In Botstiber's third volume of Pohl's Haydn biography, the Haydn aria is first mentioned on page 133, where he writes in connection with the story of the so-called "Nelson Mass":

> *Haydn verherrlichte übrigens den Sieg Nelsons bei Abukir in einer selbstständigen Komposition, in einer Tenor-Arie "Lines from the Battle of the Nile", zu welcher ihm Mrs. Knight den Text aus England gesandt hatte.*

("Incidentally Haydn glorifies Nelson's victory at Aboukir in an independent composition, a tenor aria [!] 'Lines from the Battle of the Nile', the text of which Mrs. [!] Knight had sent him from England [!]").[24]

On page 165 Botstiber quotes the previously mentioned letter by Griesinger to Breitkopf & Härtel, dated Vienna, 21st January 1801, that is to say a few months after the visit to Eisenstadt: *Haydn komponierte damals ein englisches Loblied auf Nelson und seinen Sieg; Milady Knight, Begleiterin der Hamilton, hatte den Text gemacht,* (" Haydn at that time composed an English song of praise to Nelson and his victory; Milady Knight, companion of Lady Hamilton had written the words".).

On page 335 *die sehr breit ausgeführte Gesangsszene*

("the very broadly executed scene with aria") is especially discussed by Botstiber:

> *Dieses Stück, das für Sopran und Klavierbegleitung, teilweise von Haydn teilweise von Elssler geschrieben, in Eisenstadt liegt, dürfte mit Orchesterbegleitung Begleitung gedacht sein: Einem gross angelegten begleiteten Rezitativ ("Ausonia, trembling 'midst unnumber'd woes") folgt eine Arie, die (Allegretto) den Rhythmus*

*und Charakter einer Marschhymne hat (Text. 'Blessed leader') und rezitativisch mit dazwischen gelegten Fanfaren auf den Worten 'Eternal praise, great Nelson! to thy name, and these immortal partners of thy fame!' schliesst.*

("This piece for soprano and piano accompaniment which was copied partly by Haydn and partly by Elssler, and is kept at Eisenstadt, seems to have been intended for orchestral accompaniment: an elaborate accompanied recitative, 'Ausonia, trembling 'midst unnumber'd woes', is followed by an aria (*Allegretto*) which has the rhythm and character of a march-hymn  (Text: 'Blessed leader') and, in the form of a recitative interspersed with fanfares, it ends with the words: 'Eternal praise, great Nelson! to thy name, and these immortal partners of thy fame!')

In Pohl's surviving papers[25] there are several of the notes Botstiber had used in connection with our subject, among others a list of works which Pohl had copied for himself: *Verzeichnis von Joseph Haydns Tonwerken, welche in dem fürstlichen Musik-Archiv zu Eisenstadt sich befinden.  Ein Auszug aus den sämtlichen Inventarien der fürstlich Esterházyschen Archive für Kirchen-, Kammer- und Theatermusik vom Jahre 1825. den [...] 1864. Nach genommer Einsicht der Original-Dokumente verfertigt von Dr. Anton Kraitsch, Bürgermeister in Pottendorf.*

("List of Joseph Haydn's compositions, which are to be found in the princely music archives at Eisenstadt.  An extract from the official inventories of Prince Esterházy's archives of church, chamber, and theatre music for the year 1825. On the [...] 1864. Made by Dr. Anton Kraitsch, Mayor of Pottendorf [near Wiener Neustadt], after a study of the original documents"). Here listed as No.67 in the section "Vocal music, arias, duets" we find: "Lines from the Battle of the Nile by Miss Kinght [sic] and sat [sic] in music by Dr. Haydn. *am Clavier zu singen.  Ein Blatt ist eigenhändig von Haydn und das Ganze hier noch unbekannt.*    ("...to be sung at the piano.  One leaf is in Haydn's own hand and the whole [work] is still unknown here").  The last sentence may be by Pohl himself.  In the Haydn thematic Catalogue by Eusebius Mandyczewski, chief editor of the new complete edition of Haydn's works, the aria is also mentioned, with the note: *Halb-Autograph in Eisenstadt, Pohls Abschrifz bei mir* ("Semi-autograph at Eisenstadt, Pohl's copy with me').[26]  No mention of the aria is made in the list of works[27] compiled with Haydn's help, by his factotum Johann Elssler.  It is however mentioned in the list of Haydn's music library which Elssler[28] made a little later (about 1808).[29]

Here it is listed[30] among the music, written in unknown hands: "Lines from the Battle of the Nile by Miss Knight, and set in Musik by Dr Haydn, *bey den Pianoforte zu singen"* ("to be sung to the pianoforte").  This evidently is the copy that came to Esterházy with the other Haydn music after his death.

The only surviving manuscript of the aria was originally at Eisenstadt; it is now at Budapest,[31] where it was sent together with the rest of Haydn's music, all of which Prince Esterházy bought at the auction held after the master's death in Vienna. (This manuscript, however, is not mentioned in the sale catalogue of Haydn's "art treasures"). The correct title of the manuscript is as follows: "Lines from the Battle of the Nile by Miss Knight and set in Musik by Dr. Haydn." This title is written by the violinist Anton Polzelli, the son of Haydn's lady friend who was a singer engaged at the Esterházy's private theatre. (It is conceivable that Polzelli was Haydn's son, he certainly was his pupil). Haydn's handwriting is evident only in the correction made to the name 'Knight' (perhaps from 'Kinght"). Added to the title is the following pencilled note, also in Polzelli's hand: *Das Fr. [Fräulein] Michaele sagt dass dies ein Schiffergesang sey und bemerkte dass es schade wäre wenn Du lieber Schwager einen Takt auslassen oder [verändern] möchtest.*

("Fräulein Michaele[32] says that this is a sailor's song and that it would be a pity if you, dear brother-in-law, were to leave out or [alter] one bar"). It is difficult to guess what this note means; it leads to the conclusion that there must have been another copy. Of the Esterházy manuscript the Recitative is in Polzelli's hand, with several corrections by Haydn; the first two pages of the aria itself are written entirely by Haydn, in a very fine small hand;[33] the rest is by Johann Elssler, and from the third page onwards only the words are written by Haydn. This is a very mixed and therefore imperfect manuscript, possibly reconstructed from Haydn's sketches, and not made from the fair copy of the whole work. Haydn obviously gave the fair copy to Lady Hamilton in Vienna. After she brought it to England, it has since disappeared.

Haydn used but nine of the 17 pages of Miss Knight's poem for his Aria, in the following order; Nos. 3, 4, 5, 8, 9, 14, 11, 15, 16, and at the end, No.11 a second time. All of the verses except No.9 were slightly modified or altered. Miss Knight herself possibly made the alterations for Haydn, or perhaps he altered them with her knowledge. It is interesting, however, that she had no written version with her (nor could she memorise one) when she quoted the only unaltered verse, No.9 in her autobiography.

In 1931 Ludwig Landshoff, who used Pohl's copy for his edition, published the aria as No.2 of the *"Edition Adler"* in Berlin. The title reads: *Nelson-Arie, Gesang von der Schlacht am Nile, Lines from the Battle of the Nile. Englischer Text von Mrs. Knight, Deutsch von Franz Hessel und L.Landshoff.* The editor, a distinguished choral-conductor who specialized, among other things, in Haydn's songs and choruses, also made an edition with an orchestral accompaniment for the aria which was published, together with the piano-edition, by the same firm. There are some additional dynamic and tempo markings, etc., which are sparingly noted in the hand-written copy, but the spelling mistakes in the text are sometimes repeated (e.g. "contest" instead of "confest", "naughty France" instead of "haughty France"). It is presumed in the preface that the aria had not previously been printed. At that time the present author held the same belief. This was not so however.

In 1913 the British Museum[34] bought, what is now known to be the first edition - and, as it would seem, the only existing copy.[35] This edition was obviously made from Haydn's lost fair copy, with all the necessary indications for the correct execution of the music;[36] the words show most of the same deviations from the printed poem as those present in the manuscript at Esterházy's (i.e. that written by Polzelli, Haydn and Elssler). The authentic first edition bears the title: "Battle of the Nile, a Favorite Cantata, with an Accompaniment for the Piano Forte, the Words by Mrs Knight, The Music Composed & Dedicated to Lady Hamilton, By Dr Haydn. Entd at Sta. Hall. Price 3s, London. Printed by Clementi, Banger, Hyde, Collard & Davis - No 26, Cheapside. (late Longman & Broderip)", and comprises 13 unnumbered folio pages. This music, printed in about 1802, was thus published during the lifetime of all the four persons so closely connected with its creation. Haydn, however, does not seem to have preserved a copy, if indeed he ever received one, for it was not among his collection of music sold after his death.

The fact that Nelson presented people with a poem that glorified himself and that Lady Hamilton sang the aria to the hero of her life, if only in private circles, is a distinctly curious feature of their journey.

In order better to judge the nature and quality of Haydn's aria in praise of Nelson let us quote Alfred Einstein's review of the Landshoff edition, as printed in the *Zeitschrift für Musikwissenschaft*, March, 1932:

> *Es ist ein Gelegenheitswerk, aber ein Gelegenheitswerk Haydns, der Entstehungszeit zwischen den beiden Oratorien durchaus würdig und mit dem Stil der grossen Rezitative von "Schöpfung" und "Jahreszeiten" verwandt. Eine schwer gehaltene Einleitung, Adagio c-moll; tief lastende, schwarze Wolken; dann heroisches Rezitativ; bei der Ankündigung Nelsons, des "intrepid warrior" eine helle und entschiedene Marschmelodie, die als eine Art Leitmotiv wiederkehrt und zum Schluss mit noch freundlicheren, kantablen Klängen, mit Fanfaren und stolzen Unisoni zu einer Art Siegessinfonie mit Singstimme sich erweitert. Voran geht eine kurze, schlagende Schlachtschilderung; die Elemente des ganzen Werkes kehren in Beethovens schwächstem und einst populärstem Werk gesteigert und verstärkt, aber so getreu wieder, dass man annehmen möchte, er habe das Stück Haydns gekannt - hätte nicht alles Militärisch-Musikalische damals in der Luft gelegen.*

("It is an occasional work, but it is an occasional work by Haydn, quite worthy of the period between the two Oratorios and related in style to the great recitatives of the "Creation" and the "Seasons". A heavy introduction, Adagio in C-minor; hovering black clouds, then the heroic recitative; an introduction of Nelson, the "intrepid warrior", a light and decided march melody which returns as a kind of theme and at the end, with friendlier singing tones, with fanfares, and proud unisons broadens into a kind of vocal victory-symphony. It is preceded by a short, vivid description of the battle; the elements of the whole work are reflected with striking likeness but with more spirit and strength in Beethoven's most feeble but once most popular work,[37] that one would presume he had known Haydn's compositions - if it were not for the fact that all military music was then in the air.") Einstein, who in 1932 called Haydn's aria *ein Abfallsprodukt oder einen Nachall der Nelson-Messe und eine Art Vorläufer von Beethovens "Schlacht von Vittoria"*

("a rubbishy work or an echo of the Nelson Mass, and a kind of forerunner of Beethoven's 'Battle of Vittoria'"), later published in the "Monthly Musical Record" (December 1934) an essay entitled "Haydn, Mozart and English Sea Heroes".

Let us here insert a note written by Dr. Andreas Bertolini, assistant of the Viennese Doctor von Malfatti, to Otto Jahn in 1852, the link between Nelson and Beethoven during the years 1806 to 1816:

> *Den ersten Gedanken zur Sinfonie Eroica gab Beethoven Bonapartes Zug nach Aegypten, und das Gerucht von Nelsons Tod in der Schlacht bei Abukir veranlasste den Trauermarsch.*

("Buonaparte's march on Egypt gave Beethoven the first idea for the 'Eroica', and the rumour of Nelson's death in the battle at Aboukir inspired the Funeral March.") But Karl Czerny wrote to Jahn:

> *Nach der Angabe von Beethovens langjährigem Freunde Dr. Bertolini gab ihm der Tod des englischen Generals Abercrombie die erste Idee zur Sinfonie Eroica. Daher der navale (nicht landmilitärische) Charakter des Themas und des ganzen ersten Satzes.*

("Beethoven's old friend Dr. Bertolini states that Beethoven's Eroica Symphony was inspired by the death of the English General Abercrombie.[38] This accounts for the naval, (and not military) character of the subject and the whole of the first movement."). The Beethoven biographical literature has put an end to these legends.[39]

After Nelson's first visit to a Vienna theatre he does not seem to have gone to the *Burgtheater* again. Whether he ever went to the Court Theatre, the *Kärntnertor Theater*, remains uncertain. In any case reference should be made to a report by Harrison:[40] "So attractive was our hero, wherever he went, that his presence drew all the best company thither: and the proprietors of the several theatres, alarmed at his lordship confining himself for a few nights to one of them in particular, protested all the rest were deserted; and that they should be entirely ruined, unless he kindly condescended to visit them by turns, which he accordingly promised, and faithfully performed. We know that Nelson and Lady Hamilton were at the *Leopoldstädter Theater* his favourite stage, on five occasions. He does not seem really to have kept his promise to visit the other private theatres i.e. the *Freihaus-* and *Josephstädter-Theater*.

Another of Harrison's[41] reports concerning Eisenstadt deserves to be mentioned: "A grand concert, too, was given in the Chapel Royal, under the direction of the chief musician, Haydn; whose famous piece, called the "Creation", was performed on this occasion, in a style worthy of that admirable composer, and particularly gratifying to those distinguished amateurs of musical science, Sir William Hamilton and his most accomplished lady. The Prince and Princess had a few years before, during a residence of several months at Naples received such polite attention from, and been so splendidly entertained by Sir William and his lady, that they repeatedly promised to evince their gratitude should the opportunity ever offer; which now happily occured, and was nobly embraced, to the extreme gratification of all parties." Nothing more is known of the Esterházy's visit to Naples; we do know, however, that a distant relative of theirs, Count Franz Esterházy, had been Austrian ambassador there since 1792. Possibly, it was he who introduced the two couples; in any case, the meeting eventually proved to the mutual advantage of Nelson and Haydn.

It remains doubtful whether the "Creation" was in reality performed in Eisenstadt at that time. This work which was first produced in Vienna in 1798, had in fact been performed once in Hungary in 1800, i.e. on March 8th, at the Royal Palace at Ofen, on the evening preceding the birthday of the Archduke Joseph, the Palatin (Viceroy) of Hungary, There is no mention of a repetition at Eisenstadt in 1800, except in Harrison's report. On the other hand, a copy of this work (which was published the same year in Vienna by Haydn himself) was found among the possessions of Lady Hamilton and was exhibited in 1932 at the London Museum.[42] On the fly leaf of Lady Hamilton's copy is the following inscription:- "In Remembrance of Milady! Vienna 23rd Aug. 1800. Your most humble & obedient Servant Leopold de Herz"; below which in Emma's own hand:- "Emma Hamilton/ Given to Her at Vienna/ Aug 23rd 1800".[43] This appears to be the first indirect contact of Lady Hamilton with Haydn in Vienna. The donor of the copy who is not to be found among the list of subscribers, was a banker and wholesale merchant of whom we shall hear more at a later stage.

Having satisfied ourselves that Haydn met Lady Hamilton and Nelson again, on the second occasion in Vienna when he gave them the new aria, it is to be presumed that their farewell took place in that City and not at Eisenstadt. If Haydn handed over the manuscript on September 22nd, this probably took place at the inn in the *Graben* where he evidently dined with the English party. However since they postponed their departure, maybe for a second time on September 23rd, the final farewells probably took place on the 24th or 25th, at Haydn's house. We suggest this place because Haydn probably went through the aria with Lady Hamilton himself in his home, where several pianos were available. The following scene was definitely laid in Vienna, and not in Haydn's country house at Eisenstadt.[44] Griesinger relates in his *Biographische Notizen* (page 105 etc.) : *Als Lord Nelson durch Wien reiste, bat er sich eine abgenützte Feder aus, welch Haydn bei seinen Kompositionen gedient hatte, und er verehrte ihm dagegen seine Uhr.*

("When Lord Nelson travelled through Vienna, he asked Haydn for an old worn out pen which Haydn had used for his compositions, and in exchange gave him his watch").[45] But on page 110 Griesinger goes on:

> Seinem Bruder Michael in Salzburg (gestorben den 8ten August 1806) hatten die Franzosen im Jahr 1800 seine wenige Baarschaft und zwey silberne Uhren genommen. Haydn schickte ihm dafür eine goldne Uhr und Dose, und versprach auch Geld, sobald seine Interessen einlaufen würden.

(" The French at Salzburg in [December] 1800 took from his brother Michael (who died on August 8th, 1806) the little cash he possessed and two silver watches. Haydn therefore sent him a gold watch and a box, and also promised to send money as soon as his interest came to hand"). As it seems that Nelson's watch was not found among Haydn's personal belongings,[46] it is likely that he had given it away; not, as it is suggested, three months after he received it, but rather in the late summer of 1801, when his brother, the Salzburg church composer, came to see him again. Nelson likewise does not seem to have preserved Haydn's pen, for that, like the autograph of Haydn's aria, was lost in England.

Nelson sat for a painter and a sculptor while he was in Vienna. The painting and the bust were later sent to him in London and are now in public ownership. They were executed by two highly gifted Austrian artists: the painter became famous far beyond the boundaries of his own country, but the sculptor was soon forgotten even at home.

Friedrich Heinrich Füger, mentioned earlier in connection with Mrs. St. George, was famous in his time as an historical painter and as the illustrator of Klopstock's epic Die Messiade. He lived in Naples from 1781 until 1783, as protegé of the connoisseur Count Franz de Paula Lamberg, who was then the Austrian ambassador. Füger painted four allegorical frescoes on the ceilings of the Queen's library at Caserta. Towards the end of the 19th century when it was realised what treasures had been hidden in Austrian miniature paintings, Füger became posthumously famous. Next to Daffinger, whose colours are richer, he now ranks as the best master of this art that Austria has produced, and is called "The German Cosway". His composition and his colours are much finer than is usually the case on ivory. His portraits, male as well as female, are very spiritualised, for instance that of the three Countesses Thun (1788) which Lord Minto knew and admired.[47] The tendency to treat all his models in this fashion results in a suggestion of unreality. Nevertheless hardly any of his genuine miniatures leave one indifferent, they all excite the beholder, and some it must be said are unforgettable. But it must be borne in mind, that Füger - like Daffinger - although we know them only from coloured engravings, came under the influence of the great English portrait painters, especially that of Gainsborough.

Füger, director of the Vienna Academy of Art, painted Nelson's portrait in

*Monument erected by Maria Carolina in the park at Schönbrunn, with a medallion by Thaller representing her children and an inscription commemorating her happy childhood.*

Vienna, but on whose recommendation he came to receive the commission which Nelson had given and paid for himself, we do not know. But since Füger often painted Queen Maria Carolina,[48] who knew him in Naples, and other members of the Imperial Family, it can be presumed that she recommended the artist to Nelson. On looking at this portrait in oils[49] (which although it hangs in the National Portrait Gallery in London is not sufficiently well-known) we find Nelson in civilian clothes, possibly a housecoat which he wore at the inn on the *Graben* in Vienna. His face, three quarter profile turned to the left, is more like that of a philosopher than an admiral, which is not surprising if the description by the anonymous Hungarian journalist[50] is accurate. The great man is unflatteringly portrayed deep in thought, his nose and mouth of realistic size and shape, his thinning hair arranged in no artificial style; and yet the spirit of this "Hero in a Dressing Gown" is evident in every detail. As this picture produces an effect so different from L.F. Abbott's, or for that matter all the other heroic Nelson portraits, we are inclined to believe that this is the real Nelson, and not the usual artistic idealisation of a hero. However valuable this picture may be as a work of art and especially as tangible evidence in the story of this episode in Nelson's life, one must remember the fact that great artists and especially great painters often misrepresent great men; e.g. Waldmüller, the master of Austrian painters, strangely misrepresented Beethoven. One may however say that this is undoubtedly one of the best portraits of Nelson.

To this document in oil we can add a written one: a letter from Nelson to the Viennese banker and wholesale merchant, Leopold von Herz, whose house Wellington, the other English conqueror of Napoleon, frequented during the Vienna Congress in 1815. His father, Salomon von Herz, was the founder of the wholesale concern, of which Samuel and Ignaz Markus Leidesdorfer later became shareholders.[51] Leopold von Herz who was born at Hamburg in 1767 and died in 1828, was, besides being an amateur poet, also a partner in the banking firm of Offenheimer & Herz. As Metternich's confidential agent in money affairs he was concerned with the English subsidies, and the Chancellor himself introduced him to Wellington at a luncheon, on the day of the latter's arrival in Vienna (February 2nd, 1815). Wellington's predecessor, Castlereagh, was also present at that luncheon.[52]

Nelson's note to Herz[53] is addressed to (outside):- "Mr Hartz / Banker at / Vienna / BNN", and reads (inside): "Vienna Sept 23rd 1800. Whenever Mr Füger delivers to Mr. Hertz the Banker three Pictures Viz. One full length of the Queen of Naples. One full length of Lady Hamilton & one quarter of a length of Lord Nelson of the Nile: Then Mr. Hertz is to pay Mr. Füger the sum of two hundred and fifty pounds sterling, for which Mr. Hertz will have the goodness to draw bills on Lord Nelson in London - Bronte Nelson of the Nile". It is addressed and signed by Nelson himself, the text of the letter, however, is in a strange hand, perhaps Oliver's. Although it is obvious that Nelson's pen once again gave him some trouble, the mark below the address is not to be mistaken for an inkblot; in the original it is to be recognized as Nelson's seal. Round the coat of arms is Nelson's motto "Faith and Works", and in the centre the more significant and well-known motto of the Order of the Bath, *Tria juncta in uno*.

The three pictures, which Nelson had ordered, were not ready when he left Vienna; the portrait of the Queen was perhaps not begun. Apparently no Füger portrait of her or of Lady Hamilton ever reached England; we must therefore presume that Füger did not finish these two pictures. It is to be regretted that among the many portraits of Lady Hamilton, by Morghen, Reynolds, Romney, Tischbein, Kaufmann and Vigée-Le Brun there is none by Füger. Even the sketch he made has either been destroyed or remains unrecognized. He had also painted the King of Naples, and this oil portrait is at the Haydn Museum in Vienna.

It is not known when Füger sent his half-length portrait of Nelson to London nor when Herz settled his account.

Thaller, the sculptor for whom Nelson sat in Vienna, like Füger was known to the Queen of Naples. Franz Thaller, born at Wörgl in Tyrol in 1759, was sculptor to the Royal Imperial Collection of Antiques. He was also a Taxidermist for the Royal Imperial Natural History Collection. It was he who in 1796 undertook for this collection the gruesome task of preserving and stuffing the body of Angelo Soliman a Moor who had accepted the Christian faith, was baptized in Vienna and who was a member of one of the City's Masonic Lodges.[54] After he had finished the Nelson bust, Thaller portrayed many famous people including the Queen of Naples, Haydn and Wellington. The Queen is shown in a group with four of her children in a bronze medallion en relief. This medallion is still to be seen on that strange monument which stands in the park of Schönbrunn, near the former playground of Maria Theresa's children, used in those days by the Princesses of Naples, and later probably by the Duke of Reichstadt, Napoleon's son. This monument consists of a cubical granite plinth circle surmounted by a classical bronze vase. On the front of the pedestal is the medallion, on the back a bronze plate with the following inscription which apparently was composed by the Queen herself:-

*Der kindlichen Zaertlichkeit für die unsterbliche Maria Theresia / der Liebe zum theuern Vaterlande / der frohen Rueckerinnerung an jede Freude der sorgenfreyen Jugend widmete dieses laendliche Denkmal auf dem Platze / den sie einst als Kind pflegte / nun in dem Kreise ihrer Kinder / Maria Carolina / Koeniginn Beyder Sicilien / bei ihrer Anwesenheit im Jahre MDCCCII.*

("This rural monument, dedicated in filial affection to the immortal Maria Theresa, in love to the dear Fatherland and in happy memory of every joy of a carefree childhood, at this place which she had enjoyed as a child and where is now surrounded by her own children, was erected by Maria Carolina, Queen of the Two Sicilies, during her visit in the year MDCCCII").

Although this monument was erected in 1802, after the Queen had left Vienna, Thaller did not exhibit the medallion (probably a plaster cast) at the annual exhibition of the Vienna Academy of Fine Arts until 1813 (Catalogue No. 22).[55] In 1816 the same Academy exhibited Thaller's plaster bust of Arthur, Duke of Wellesley, Duke of Wellington (Catalogue No. 15). His likeness of Haydn, made between 1790-95, is a small bust in wax, or rather there are two almost identical wax busts. They are approximately 12 inches high and are dressed in material, worn by Haydn himself; the wigs too are made of his own hair, a practice not unusual in those days.[56] One of these busts used to stand under a glass-cover in Haydn's house up to 1809 (the silk ribbon, however, is of a later date). The second bust, formerly belonging to Rusloff von Vivenot, and now in the *Kunsthistorisches Museum*, Vienna, is slightly lighter than the other. The composition of the two busts in polychrome adds to their lifelike appearance.

And now to Thaller's bust of Nelson. It is still in the possession of the Admiral's family. A copy of the bust, once in the gallery of the Greenwich Hospital, is now at the National Maritime Museum. The 1922 catalogue of the exhibition at the "Painted Hall of Greenwich Hospital, and the Royal Naval Museum, Greenwich" (p.62) describes the piece as "Plaster cast of a bust in possession of Earl Nelson, executed in Vienna, in 1800, by Franz Thaller and Matthias Ranson". Apparently Thaller himself only took a plaster cast from his clay model; this cast later came to London where it was copied in marble by Ranson in 1801. The copyist, no doubt, does not capture all the good points of the original. Nelson is shown in full dress, the loss of his right arm is stressed by the rendering of the empty sleeve. The whole work is somewhat stiff although in the face there is a trace of the same greatness which Füger transferred to his canvas in so masterly a fashion. But it is unfair to judge Thaller's work when it is seen only through Ranson's copy. Since the body (with the uniform) of Thaller-Ranson's bust is identical with that of Flaxman's later Nelson bust,[57] it seems that Thaller sent the head only - or a cast of Nelson in civilian dress - and that Ranson provided the body for both busts. (The bases of the two busts differ slightly). "Pearson's Magazine" (London) published a "Special Nelson centenary number" in October, 1905 which contains[58] an essay "On the Nelson Portraits" by Horatio, Third Earl Nelson: " ... The next likeness in order brings us to the beautiful bust modelled at Vienna during Nelson's overland journey home. The inscription at the back reads: Franz Thaller and Matthias Ranson, Vienna MDCCI, - a date which is short of a C, for MDCCCI. was evidently the date of the work. This bust and its pedestal were at Merton. They were obtained for me from Miss Pettigrew, the daughter of Dr. Pettigrew, F.R.S., who received it for professional services to Mrs. Alderman Smith. - "This bust must be taken as the ruling guide to all likenesses of the Admiral. With the full-length Abbott, it reminds me much of my Great-Aunt Catherine,[59] Nelson's youngest and favourite sister." Iconography (as the science of portraiture) is really not a science at all but more a matter of feeling. But we are indebted to Thaller and Füger - the two Austrian artists - for their contributions to our knowledge of the hero's physiognomy.

It is not known who ordered or paid for this bust, but there are accounts of Nelson's expenditures in Vienna which we shall list. In the Supplement of "The Collection of Autograph Letters and Historical Documents, formed by Alfred Morrison (Second Series, 1882-1893"), A. W. Thibaudeau has catalogued "The Hamilton and Nelson Papers". The 2nd volume which covers the period from 1798 to 1815 (London 1894) includes, on p.105, a letter by Captain Alexander

Ball, Governor of Malta, to Lord Nelson, dated Malta, 27th September 1800, by which time our party had already left Vienna: "We have heard unfavourable reports of Sir William Hamilton's health, which I hope you will be able to contradict; we hear that Lady Hamilton remains with the Queen at Vienna." We mention this rumour here only as a point of interest; on p.390 of the catalogue we find under the title "N. [Nelson] in Account with Messrs. Marsh, Page & Creed":

1800:

| | | | |
|---|---|---|---|
| "8th Oct. To paid Bill to Hoffenheimer & Kerr | £260 | 0 | 0 |
| [*recte:* Offenheimer & Herz] | | | |

Then on p. 392

| | | | |
|---|---|---|---|
| "30th Oct. To 1st Bill to Ofenheimer & Hertz 7th [Nov] | £100 | 0 | 0 |
| "    "    To 1st Bill to ditto 4th [Nov] | £200 | 0 | 0 |
| "    "    To 1st Bill to ditto 4th [Nov] | £300 | 0 | 0 |
| 15th Nov. To paid Draft to Mr. Oliver | £ 34 | 10 | 9 |
| 20th  "    To paid Bill on you by Ofenheimer - | | | |
| & Hertz | £113 | 19 | 0" |

And on p. 394

| | | | |
|---|---|---|---|
| "1801 22nd Sept. To Bill by Offenheimer & Co | | | |
| to Harman & Co, 2nd April | £348 | 0 | 0" |

Turning to the appendix on p. 401 - we find under the title "Sheets of Accounts (in Lord Nelson's writing), dated between July 20th and September 21st, 1802":

"Subscribed Sir Wm. Hamilton & myself at Merton July 20th, 1802. £100 each, being £200."

And again on p. 404

| | | |
|---|---|---|
| "£1094 | 2 4 | Half the expense of the journey to England. |
| 255 | 0 0 | Lent on the Road. |
| 927 | 14 0 | At Palermo. |
| 2276 | 16 4 | Owing Ld N. |
| 957 | 19 3 | |
| 1218 | 17 1 | Due Ld N. [obviously £1318.17.1] |
| 62 | 8 1 | Owing Sir Wm. Hamilton. |
| 1156 | 9 0 | |
| 52 | 10 0 | |
| 1103 | 19 0 | |

Merton Sept. 21st, 1802."

Further on p. 404:

"Money drawn for by Lord Nelson.

| | | | | |
|---|---|---|---|---|
| Vienna | Aug. 19th | 100 | 0 | 0 |
| | 21st | 100 | 0 | 0 |
| | 22nd | 300 | 0 | 0 |
| | Sept. 13th | 200 | 0 | 0 |
| | 21st | 300 | 0 | 0 |
| | 23rd | 100 | 0 | 0 |
| Prague | 29th | 100 | 0 | 0 |
| ......Mr. Oliver [Nov. 15th] | | 34 | 10 | 9" |

And finally on p. 405

"Drawn for and paid out by Ld N. between
July 13th & Nov. 18th £ 3431 16 0.

| | | | | |
|---|---|---|---|---|
| Spent by Lord Nelson. | | | | |
| | Sept. 13th | £111 | 10 | 0 |
| | to 21st | 100 | 0 | 0 |
| | | | | |
| Sir W. Hamilton. | | | | |
| to | Sept 13th | £205 | 0 | 0 |
| Hambg. | Oct. 28th | 50 | 0 | 0 |
| | | £255 | 0 | 0 |
| | | | | |
| To be deducted from the bills drawn | | £1243 | 13 | 3 |
| | | 3431 | 16 | 0 |
| To be divided | | £2188 | 4 | 9 |
| Sir Wm. H. proportion | | 1094 | 2 | 4 |
| | | 255 | 0 | 0 |
| | Due Lord Nelson | £1349 | 2 | 4" |

Strangely enough it was not until two years later, in September 1802, that the two friends made arrangements for settling the expenses of the journey.[60]

Having parted from Haydn who lived half-way to Schönbrunn, next followed their adieux to Maria Carolina at Schönbrunn, probably on September 24th or 25th. Harrison writing of this time has something to say[61] about the party's expenses: "Though the Queen of Naples insisted on defraying all sorts of expenses incurred by his lordship and friends during their stay at Vienna, where they had so handsomely escorted her - and who had accordingly everything prepared for them at the palace, and regularly sent - they constantly purchased,[62] without her Majesty's knowledge whatever they might happen to want." He continues[63] :- "At the earnest request of the Queen of Naples, their departure from Vienna had been put off for several days; when it could not longer be protracted, this dreaded separation took place at the Imperial Palace of Schönbrunn, situated on the river Wien, which gives name to the city of Vienna[64], from where the Palace is only two miles distant. The Queen was prodigiously affected, and earnestly entreated Lady Hamilton to return with her to Naples. Sir William, too, Her Majesty remarked, when he had his business in England, where he was for that purpose accompanying his illustrious friend, would find the soft climate of Italy far more congenial to his constitution than the damp atmosphere of his own native country.[65] Neither Sir William nor his lady, however, could listen to any arrangement which must subject them to even a temporary separation from each other. Their domestic happiness notwithstanding the very considerable disparity of age, was ever most exemplary; and it seems probable, that the amiable demeanour of Lady Hamilton, whose tender regard for Sir William could not fail to excite the admiration of every virtuous visitor, first gave birth to that ardent friendship by which Lord Nelson unquestionably felt himself attached to her ladyship. When the Queen of Naples found, that nothing could induce Sir William to leave his lady behind, Her Majesty immediately wrote an instrument, appointing Lady Hamilton to receive, for her eminent services, an annuity of one thousand pounds a year.[66] This however, Sir William positively objected to her ladyship's accepting. He maintained, that he could not suffer his lady to take it, without subjecting them both to unmerited suspicions at home; and her ladyship impressed with similar sentiments, instantly tore the paper in pieces. The Queen of Naples, however, persisting in her desire to promote, if possible, the interests of her estimable and beloved friends, now penned an elegant epistle to Her Britannic Majesty, in which she is said to have recommended Sir William and Lady Hamilton as worthy of receiving every possible honour." Maria Carolina, as we see, intended to write a letter of recommendation to the Queen of England on September 23rd but, whether she wrote it or not, no trace of such a letter either to the Queen or to the King of England has been found. Maria Carolina could not possibly have renewed her offer to Lady Hamilton at a later date as she became impoverished after the death of Sir William and Nelson. And as the English did nothing for Emma in spite of Nelson's appeal in his Last Will and Testament Lady Hamilton was thus forsaken by both states to whom she had rendered such great service.

As the Queen stressed Sir William's health in order to persuade Lady Hamilton to return with her to Naples, we should mention the state of Nelson's health towards the end of his stay in Vienna. Harrison says:[67] "The journey, which had proved too fatiguing for his friend, Sir William Hamilton, seems to have nearly restored our hero to perfect health; who, on his first arrival at Leghorn, had been extremely indisposed, as to be four days out of seven confined to his bed. In truth, besides the salutary changes of air, in the different climates thus rapidly passed, from the excessive enervating heats and sultry breezes in Italy, to the corroborating cool temperature of the Austrian refreshing gales[68] his Lordship's ever active mind felt not only delivered from the thraldom of a controlled and perplexed command, but invigorated by the boundless admiration he beheld at each stage of his progress, and through every varying country which he travelled, affectionately and respectfully tendered to its indubitable and transcendent worth... such public testimonies of universal esteem, could not fail to exhilarate his heart, and fortify it against the depressive influence of any deficient kindness where he felt himself still more entitled to receive it. To enumerate all the instances of affectionate respect which his Lordship and friends experienced while at Vienna, would be quite an impracticable task."

In this book we have endeavoured to fill in a few of the gaps and if we have failed to "enumerate all the instances of affectionate respect" shown to the party, we have, as far as it is humanly possible, tried our best to reconstruct the story.

1 The libretto was not published until 1807 (Copy in the *Nationalbibliothek*, Vienna).

2 Pettigrew, "Memoirs and Letters of ...Nelson", I.389. (Not in Palumbo's edition of Maria Carolina's original - French - letters to Lady Hamilton.)

3 Lady Hamilton never returned to Naples.

4 "Life and Letters of...Lord Minto", III. 152.

5 "The Dispatches and Letters of...Nelson", IV. 266 et.seq.

6 "New Nelson Manuscripts. VI. Nelson's autograph letters to his wife (1800) down to his return to England". "Literature", April 9th 1898, vol. 2, no.25, p.241.

7 Alexander Davison, government contractor, prize agent and confidential friend of Nelson.

8 Another of this theatre's own playwrights.

9 The elder of two brothers. Mozart composed *Ein deutsches Kriegslied* ("A German Song of War") for Friedrich, the younger brother, in 1788. The opera did not reach the Vienna Court Theatres until 1805.

10 Raffaele Palumbo, in his *Carteggio di Maria Carolina, Regina delle due Sicilie, con Lady Emma Hamilton, Documenti inediti*...(Naples 1877, p.214 et. seq.), prints the letter after the autograph in the British Museum (vol. 1616, fol.121, Bibl. Egerton MS.) in the original French, without accents or punctuation. The English version of Pettigrew's "Nelson" (I.399 et. seq.), in which the letter is wrongly dated October 23rd 1800, is also quoted here.

11 Queen Charlotte Sophia of England.

12 The frequently mentioned ambassador of Naples to London, Fabrizio Ruffo, Prince Castelcicala, who had gone to London on a special mission.

13 Tomaso di Somma, Marquis de Circello, his successor from 1793-1800.

14 Lavinia, the eldest daughter of Charles Bingham, first Earl of Lucan, 1781 married to George John Spencer, second Earl Spencer, First Lord of the Admiralty (1794-1801).

15 On October 2nd 1798 Lady Hamilton wrote from Naples to Lady Nelson ("Dispatches", III. 138 et. seq., wrongly dated December 2nd; Sichel's "Emma Lady Hamilton", p.489): "Lady Knight and her amiable daughter desire to be remembered to your Ladyship. I hope you received the ode I sent; it is very well written, but Miss Knight is very clever in everything she undertakes." If there was a letter accompanying the ode, it has not been preserved.

16 British Museum (Add. Ms. 34990, f.99) possesses the printed textbook by the anonymous poet, 7 pages Octavo.

17 British Museum: 11602 et seq. 20/5, 12 pages Quarto; the author of this poem also remains

unknown, in spite of the initials. John Knox Laughton in his "Nelson and his Companions in Arms", London 1896, p.335, suggests that the author was an Italian on account of his bad English.

18 "Autobiography", I.151 et. seq.

19 This quotation which Miss Knight seems to have copied from an earlier version or from memory, differs in several words from the printed version of the 9th stanza and Haydn's composition.

20 Cf. the author's booklet *Mozart und die Wiener Logen*,Vienna 1932, pp.18 et. seq. and 33.

21 Reprinted in the appendix, with the correction of obvious misprints.

22 14 pages Quarto, pages 2 and 14 blank, 13 pages numbered.

23 As the dedication was not noticed at the time of purchase, this accounts for the low price at which the copy was bought.

24 The first mistake is due to Pohl, the second to Haydn himself, the third probably to Botstiber.

25 *Archiv der Gesellschaft der Musikfreunde*, Vienna.

26 Later passed to Botstiber.

27 Esterházy family archives. The list was reproduced in facsimile by Jens Peter Larsen, Copenhagen 1941.

28 The father of the famous dancer, Fanny Elssler; he went to England with Haydn in 1794/5.

29 Now in the British Museum.

30 Leaf 27, page 2, number 128.

31 Esterházy Family Archives in the National Library, Budapest.

32 Possibly a sister of the violinist at Eisenstadt, Ernst Michael.

33 Pohl dated the handwriting, which is like that of Haydn's last Mass, about 1802.

34 See Marion M. Scott's article "Haydn Relics and Reminiscences in England", "Music and Letters", April 1932, p.130.

35 H.1601. d,1.

36 There are also deviations in the music of the two printed editions which can now quite easily be compared.

37 "Wellington's Victory" or "The Battle of Vittoria", 1813, performed in London for the first time at Drury Lane Theatre on 10th February 1815. Beethoven composed this "Battle Symphony" for his intended journey to England and especially for the "Panharmonicon" which the Viennese mechanic Mälzel proposed exhibiting in this country.

38 General Sir Ralph Abercrombie who had made the landing with English troops against the French at Aboukir on 8th March 1801, was fatally wounded on 21st March in the Battle of Alexandria. Beethoven's Third Symphony was composed in 1801-1803.

39 Thayer-Deiters-Riemann, "Beethoven", 2nd volume, 3rd edition, pp.64 and 420. On page 420 it is surmised that Bertolini possibly confused Beethoven's Symphony with Kauer's PianoTrio, *Nelsons grosse Seeschlacht*.

40 "Nelson", II. 250 et. seq.

41 II.252

42 Cf. Marion M. Scott's article "Haydn's Relics and Reminscences in England", "Music and Letters", April 1932, p.130.

43 Four months later, on December 24th, 1800, Buonaparte was present at the first Paris performance of the "Creation" at the Grand Opera.

44 Michael Brenet ("Haydn", Oxford 1926, pp.57) not only shifts the scene to Eisenstadt as others did before him, but he also changes the year to 1797.

45 Compare *Allgemeine Wiener musikalische Zeitung*, Vienna, 1841, p.28.

46 The official records for 1801 of the auction of his personal belongings, preserved in the *Archiv der Stedt Wien*, mention two gold watches: one pocket watch which was bought for 390 Gulden and a minute watch which the sole heir, Haydn's nephew Matthias Fröhlich, withdrew.

47 Among them Lady Caroline Clanwilliam. Füger in 1770/1 also painted his special patron, Sir

Robert Murray Keith, the British Ambassador in Vienna.

48 Two portraits of her are reproduced in Eduard Leisching's *Das Wiener Miniatur-Bildnis*, pp.66 and 83. The portrait, painted at Naples in 1790 is now in the Naples Museum of the History of Art. Among other portraits Füger painted a group of Maria Theresa's children (about 1776), the Archduchess Clementine and the Empress Maria Theresa.

49 Füger gave up miniature painting in 1797 because of eye trouble.

50 Magyar Hírmondó, as quoted above.

51 Cf. the *Wiener Merkantil-Protokoll* at the *Archiv der Stedt Wien*, Vienna.

52 Vide: Karl Bertuch's *Tagebuch vom Wiener Kongress,* Berlin 1916, p.111. - Wellington also visited Frau von Arnstein.

53 4 quarto pages, formerly in the possession of and published by *Moderne Welt*, Vienna 1920, vol. 2 , No.4, pp.17 et. seq.) Paul Tausig of Baden, near Vienna, in 1934 advertised in the catalogue of the second-hand bookseller V. A. Heck of Vienna.

54 In the course of our story, an attentive reader may notice that the black girl, whom we met at Graz in Lady Hamilton's service, made but a transitory appearance. If the author should be asked for a possible explanation, he would hazard the following guess: Nelson sent the black girl from his inn in the *Graben* to the nearby *Hofbibliothek* to deliver the copy of Miss Knight's poem. A minor official of the library showed the black girl the stuffed body of Soliman on the top floor of the building, where the Natural History Collection was housed. The black girl, anticipating a similar fate at the hands of the white people, immediately fled back to Africa! O.E.D. - Incidentally , the stuffed body of Soliman is lost. (Note of the editors.)

55 See Cyriac von Bodenstein's *Hundert Jahre Wiener Kunstgeschichte*, Vienna 1888, p.190, and *Mitteilungen des Staatsdenkmalamtes*, Vienna 1919, I. II et. seq, where Dagobert Frey reproduced the monument.

56 Compare Nelson's wax figure by Miss Catherine Andras in Westminster Abbey.

57 United Service Club, London.

58 Vol.20 II.348 et.seq.

59 Wife of George Matcham, both of whom, after the death of Lady Hamilton, took care of her daughter, Horatia Nelson.

60 Sir William drew an annual pension of £1,200 from 1801.

61 "Nelson", II.254.

62 In part, possibly, from the money they had won at faro at Eisenstadt.

63 II. 254

64 This explanation is wrong, the river was in fact named after the city.

65 On February 7th, 1800 Hamilton had written to Nelson at Malta that he intended to return to Naples as a private individual.

66 Another version says: insured through the banking house of Fries with Vienna *Nationalbank*. John Cordy Jeaffreson questions the whole story in his "Lady Hamilton and Lord Nelson", London, 1888, pp.171 et. seq.

67 II. 251. et. seq.

68 This did not apply to Vienna during that August, as we have seen.

# CHAPTER 11
## *Departure for London Via Prague*

On Friday, September 26th, they left Vienna. The party, numbering seventeen, still included Mrs. Cadogan and Miss Knight, but in the place of Vice-Consul Anderson who probably stayed on, they were joined by Nelson's secretary, Oliver.[1] To be exact there were actually eighteen; for there was a "stowaway", Lady Hamilton's unborn child of whose existence probably only she and Nelson knew.

The journey presumably took them to Prague on the Moldau by way of Brünn (Brno) in Moravia. Once again let us quote Harrison,[2] since we know very little of their visit to that city: "The Archduke Charles[3] had written to his aunt, the Queen of Naples, after her arrival, [at Vienna], entreating that Lord Nelson might be requested to visit him at Prague, on the way to Dresden; being

*View of Prague. Nelson and his travelling companions spent a few days there, continuing their journey between Vienna and London, before embarking on the Elbe to reach Dresden by water.*

himself so extremely ill, that he was unable to pay the British hero his respects at Vienna, as had been his most earnest wish. His lordship accordingly, on arriving at Prague, the capital of Bohemia, had an immediate interview with that great military hero. He was accompanied, as usual, by his friends, Sir William and Lady Hamilton, to the palace [on the Hradschin] ; and was so delighted with the archduke, that he said when he got into the carriage returning- to their hotel - 'This is a man after my own heart!' The next day, being the anniversary of our hero's birth, Michaelmas-day 1800,[4] the Archduke Charles gave a grand entertainment; verses written for the occasion were published in the newspapers; and the whole city was illuminated, Sir William Hamilton politely remarked at this festival, with one of these two renowned heroes on each side of him, that he had then the honour to be between the greatest naval and the greatest military character in Europe. - On the following day, Lord Nelson departed for Dresden." Here it should be remembered that Archduke Charles' service situation was then similar to Nelson's: in spite of his glory, he was temporarily undergoing a period of enforced retirement - from the middle of March until the middle of December 1800 which meant that he was in disgrace.

129

Miss Knight, who once again is wrong in her dates, writes of their stay in Prague:-[5] "On the 27th of September we proceeded on our travels, and on the 'morrow arrived at Prague, where the hotel at which we alighted was splendidly illuminated in honour of Lord Nelson - the host, however, not forgetting to charge for the lights in his bill. On the 1st of October we embarked on the Elbe at Lowositz[6] and reached Dresden the following evening." The truth is that their stay at Prague probably lasted from the 27th to 30th of September.

There is however another contemporary report about these days at Prague, this time an illustrated French book which was published in London in 1826 under the title *Charles van Schorel de Wilryck, ou Le Fualdès Belge.* Charles' elder brother was the Lord Mayor of Antwerp who had died in Vienna. The book, which was probably written by himself, frequently mentions Nelson, the Hamiltons and Miss Knight, even printing part of a poem by the latter to the Archduke Charles. We learn that the party alighted at the *Schwarzen Loewen* (Black Lion)[7] hotel and the book contains a lithograph showing Nelson's birthday dinner party in that hotel. It is only a minor point that the author calls Saint Michael the patron of the hero, so thinking it was a celebration of that day; he also mistakes the year 1799 for 1800. The picture bears the following title:

> *Le Héros du Nil assistant à un banquet le 29 Sept. 1799, jour de Saint Michel, son patron, à l'hotel du Lion Noir à Prague, ou il fut adressé avec sa société, Sir et Milady Hamilton, Miss Knight, &c: à Mr C. Van Schorel, lors de son passage par cette ville se rendant de Naples et de Vienne à Londres. Parmi les Convives se trouvèrent S: E: Le Comte de Cobentzel, Ministre d'Autriche. Le Comte O'Kelly, ci-devant Ministre de l'Empereur à Dresde, Le Comte de Thiennes de Rumbeke, Mad[e] son Epouse, Soeur du sus-dit Comte de Cobentzel, Le Vicomte de Choiseul, et quelques autres pesonnages. Pendant le repas la belle Milady Hamilton chanta le beau* God save the King, *et de charmans couplets composés par l'aimable et spirituelle Miss Knight, en l'honneur du Héros.*

("While attending a banquet on September 29th 1799 in the "Black Lion" hotel in Prague, a speech was addressed to the hero of the Nile and his company, Sir and Milady Hamilton, Miss Knight, etc., by Mr. C. Van Schorel, during Nelson's stay in this town, on his way from Naples and Vienna to London. Among the guests were His Excellency the Count of Cobenzl,[8] Austrian Minister, the Count O'Kelly,[9] former Imperial Minister at Dresden, the Count of Thiennes de Rumbeke, his wife,[10] the sister of the aforementioned Count of Cobenzl, the Viscount Choiseul[11] and other personages. During the meal the lovely Lady Hamilton sang the beautiful *God save the King* and some charming stanzas written by the amiable and witty Miss Knight, in honour of the Hero").

These verses of Miss Knight's, written for Nelson's birthday, are apparently lost. The dinner at the "Black Lion" consisted among other things of "goose and apple sauce".

*Nelson's birthday was celebrated in Prague, in the 'Black Lion' hotel. The Admiral sits at the left end of the table. From van Schorel's book.*

The Elector Friedrich August III was ruling at Dresden, and Mr. Hugh Elliot, a brother of Lord Minto, was English Ambassador at the Saxon Court.[12] We must once again refer to Mrs. St. George, the young widow whose tongue was as sharp as her pen. In her "Remains" we read on p.105: "Oct.3. Dined at Mr. Elliot's with only the Nelson party.[13] It is plain that Lord Nelson thinks of nothing but Lady Hamilton, who is totally occupied by the same object ... Lady Hamilton takes possession of him, and he is a willing captive, the most submissive and devoted I have seen. Sir William is old, infirm, all admiration of his wife, and never spoke to-day but to applaud her. Miss Cornelia Knight seems the decided flatterer of the two, and never opens her mouth but to show forth their praise; and Mrs.Cadogan, Lady Hamilton's mother, is what one might expect. After dinner we had several songs in honour of Lord Nelson, written by Miss Knight, and sung by Lady Hamilton. She puffs the incense full in his face; but he receives it with pleasure, and snuffs it up very cordially. The songs all ended in the sailor's way, with 'Hip, hip, hip, hurra' and a bumper with the last drop on the nail, a ceremony I had never heard of or seen before."

It is difficult to recognise Haydn's "Nelson Aria" in this description, which was then probably performed for the first time. The "Hip, hip, hip, hurra", which as far as we know is not contained in any of Miss Knight's poems, would indicate the recital of another song e.g. "The Battle of the Nile", text by J.W.Fielding, composer unknown, which starts with the words: "Arise, arise Britannia's sons, arise .." and ends each of the four verses with the refrain "The huzza, huzza, huzza, huzza, huzza...."[14]

On October 5th, following an invitation of Lady Hamilton's, Mrs. St.George went to see Nelson in full dress, before going to Court. And on the 7th she had breakfast with Lady Hamilton (p.108): "After showing her attitudes, she sang, and I accompanied. Her voice is good, and very strong, but she is frequently out of tune; her expression strongly marked and various; but she has no shake, no flexibility, and no sweetness. She acts her songs, which I think the last degree of bad taste." On October 8th she says (p.109) :- "Dined at Madame de Loss's, wife of the Prime Minister,[15] with the Nelson party. The Electress[16] will not receive Lady Hamilton, on account of her former dissolute life." A day later we read (p.110): "A great breakfast at the Elliots', given to the Nelson party. Lady Hamilton repeated her attitudes with great effect. All the company, except their party and myself, went away before dinner; after which Lady Hamilton, who declared she was passionately fond of champagne, took such a portion of it as astonished me. Lord Nelson was not behindhand, called more vociferously than usual for songs in his own praise, and after many bumpers, proposed the Queen of Naples, adding, 'She is my Queen; she is a Queen to the backbone.' Poor Mr. Elliot ..". Nelson's portrait was painted again in Dresden; but the pastel-portrait made by the Court painter, Johann Heinrich Schmidt (1749-1829), who painted Lady Hamilton as well, bears the date 1801.[17] It was sold by auction at Stargardt's in Berlin on May 5th 1938.[18]

On October 10th the party sailed again up the river Elbe via Magdeburg to Hamburg, where they arrived on the 21st and where, among other people, they met Gellert, well-known for his fables in verse. Miss Knight, who translated some of his poems into English, also writes in her autobiography (I.117): "The celebrated German poet Klopstock was also settled at Hamburg. We went to visit him ... Mrs.Cadogan and I supped one evening with Klopstock and his [second] wife ... He read to me also passages of his 'Messiah', and his room was hung with drawings by Füger, of subjects taken from that poem."

To follow the travellers on the final stages of their protracted journey from Naples to London: On October 31st, they went aboard the mail-packet "King George" where they were joined by Lord Whitworth, who had attended Suvorov's funeral in Moscow in May. Their departure from Hamburg, however was delayed another five days by unfavourable winds. They landed at Great Yarmouth on November 6th, after a stormy crossing, finally arriving in London on the 8th. At long last the homeland acclaimed its hero, more than two years after his first great victory. Alas, Lady Hamilton, celebrated on the Continent as the Goddess of Victory, who bathed in the hero's reflected glory and shared the admiration of Nelson's admirers, once back in her native land receded into the background.

To accord with Nelson's wishes, his wife had not met him in Yarmouth, but was awaiting him, together with his father, in Nerot's Hotel (King Street, St. James's), where preparation had also been made beforehand for Sir William and Lady Hamilton. Mrs. Cadogan and Miss Knight travelled from Yarmouth to Colchester. Thus ended the journey.

*View of London. Nelson reached his homeland on 8 November 1800. Lady Hamilton, up till then the 'unconsecrated consort of an uncrowned potentate', now had to step into the background.*

1 See Harrison, "Nelson", II.256.

2 Ibidem, II. pp. 256 et. seq.

3 The famous Austrian General (a brother of the Emperor Franz), who in 1809 was the first to beat Napoleon on land, near Aspern and Essling. Heinrich Kleist in a eulogy calls him "The Conqueror of the Unconquerable".

4 29th September.

5 Autobiography , I. 153.

6 Lobositz, North of Prague, in Bohemia.

7 Near the *Karmelitergasse*, in the *Grünes Ziegenbock-Plätzchen*.

8 Johann Philipp, Count Cobenzl, *Vizehofmeister* (Vice Chamberlain) and *Staatskanzler* (Chancellor). He had come especially from Carlsbad.

9 Probably Festus, Count O'Kelly, whose father was born in Dublin.

10 Karl Theodor Count Thiennes de Rumbeke; Marie Karoline, née Cobenzl (1755-1812), an excellent pianist and a pupil of Mozart.

11 Knight of Malta; probably Marie-Gabriel-Florent-August, Comte de Choiseul-Gouffrier, a diplomat.

12 This same Elliot later became British Ambassador in Naples, as successor to Paget, predecessor of Amherst, who in turn was followed by Bentinck.

13 Nelson stayed at the "Hotel Pologne" where Mozart also lodged on his journey to Berlin in 1789.

14 Printed copy in the British Museum, published by Bland & Weller [1798]. In the University Library, Cambridge, there also exists the text only for a variant: "Brave Sons of Spain, arise", and another: "Death of General Abercrombie", in which Nelson's name is mentioned.

15 Johann Adolf von Loss (1731-1811), from 1790 Foreign Minister of the Electorate of Saxony.

16 Amalie, nee Princess von Pfalz-Zweibrücken.

17 Emma's pastel, dated 1800, was reproduced in colours on Nov.11th 1943 in "The Illustrated London News" (p.18); Nelson's portrait (in Greenwich Museum) is reproduced in E.M. Keate's "Nelson's Wife", London 1939.

18 Schmidt's larger Nelson portrait (oil, 1808) is reproduced as frontispiece in R.H. Holme's "Horatio Nelson: England's Sailor Hero", London 1905. The unfinished portrait of a lady reproduced on p.107 of Holme's book and called Lady Hamilton, by Schmidt, is doubtful.

# CHAPTER 12
## *Epilogue*

**Finale**

Having followed the travellers to their journey's end, let us return once more to Vienna, and see what after-effects the visit of our three friends produced in that city.

On October 4th 1800 Princess Esterházy, probably the hostess at Eisenstadt, wrote a letter to Lady Hamilton which was forwarded by Hertz to Dresden. It was published with the doubtful signature "J.Fettel Esterházy", in a curious pamphlet[1] containing a number of obviously mispelt names in both languages, the original French and the editor's English translation (corrected here):

> *Vienna, ce 4e 8bre, 1800. - J'ai apris, chère Mylady, avec bien du plaisir, par Me. de Rombeh, votre heureuse arrivée à Prague. Vous avez eu si mauvais tems le premiers jours de votre voiage, que je craignois fort que le santé de mon cher Chevalier Hamilton n'en souffrit. J'ai été bien flatté, chère amie, de votre souvenir, et des assurances d'amitié dont vous avez bien voulu charger les Hobeners, pour moi. Soiez persuadée que vous existerez toujours dans mon coeur et dans mon souvenir, et que jamais je n'oublierai l'obligéante amitié que vous avez bien voulu me témoigner, et l'attachement que vous voulez bien conserver à mon frère. Tous les éloges que vous, le Chevalier, et le héros Nelson ont fait de mon frère, ont pénétré mon ame de réconnoissance. Dites, je vous prie, à ces deux messieurs, mille choses tendes de ma part, je ne cesserai de faire des voeux pour leur bonheur et leur conservation. Je vous fais mon compliment de la prise de Malthe par vos braves compatriotes. Je voulois vous en mander d'abord la nouvelle, mais je scais que l'on vous a envoié une estafette qui auroit prévenue de beaucoup ma lettre. Il s'est passé bien des événements, chère Lady, depuis votre départ,- celui de l'heureux retour de l'Empereur, et de la prolongation de l'armistique, m'a fait grand plaisir, quoique la cession des trois fortresses, par laquelle nous l'avons acheté, soit un grand rabat - joie, mais il n'y a rien que je ne préfère à la guerre. Vous saurez déjà que Thugot a resigné il y dix jours, et que l'on a accepté sa demission, mais son successeur n'a pas été nommé, et rien n'a encore été intimé légalement, ainsi nous sommes encore dans le doute de ce qui arrivera. Je me plais à croire que mon frère quittera Palerme demain, quoique je n'aie la-dessus aucune certitude, car, depuis le courier qui a aporté la nouvelle des couches de la Princesse héritière, je n'ai plus*

*eu de lettres. Notre chère et adorable Reine a été fort occupée ces jours ci, ses filles ont, je crois, chanté hier un opéra avec le Grand Duc, pour féter L'Empereur, et aujourd'hui toute la famille Imp. et Nap. dine à Saxenbourg. La Reine va quelquefois au thé,tre mais pas souvent. Je crois qu'ils ne quitteront Schönbrunn qu'après la Ste. Thérèse. Je vous avoue que je ne trouve pas bon visage à notre chère Reine; peut-être que mon attachement pour elle me la fait voir avec plus d'inquiétude que d'autres. Je voudrai la savoir toujours parfaitement heureuse, bien portante, et pouvoir la rendre, s'il étois possible, immortelle; elle meritant bien de l'être. Pour des nouvelles intéressantes, chère amie, je ne saurois vous en mander, mais je n'ai pu me refuser le plaisir de me rapeller à votre souvenir, et celui de vous souhaiter du beautems et de la santé pour la continuation de votre voiage. Puissiez vous arriver bientôt et heureusement en Angleterre. Je me berce aussi déjà de l'espoir flateur de vous revoir de retour ici au printems: en attendant, pensez un peu à moi, belle aimable Mylady, et comptez toujours sur la reconnoissance et le tendre attachement de votre affectioné ami,*

*J. Fettel Esterházy.*

*Mes complimens, s'il vous plait, à Miss Reay, et mille tendresses au Chevalier et à Mylord.*

("Vienna, October 4th, 1800.) - It was with great pleasure that I heard from Mme.de Rumbeke[2] of your safe arrival in Prague. The weather was so bad during the first few days of your journey, that I was much alarmed lest the health of dear Sir [William] Hamilton would suffer. I was extremely flattered, my dear friend, at your remembrance of me, and at the assurances of friendship you sent by the Rumbekes.[3] For my part, I can assure you that you will always exist in my heart and in my memory, and that I shall never forget your friendship to me and the attachment you entertain towards my brother.[4] The great praise that you, the Knight, and the hero Nelson have bestowed on my brother fills my heart with gratitude. I beg you to remember me kindly to both those gentlemen; I shall never cease to pray for their happiness and preservation. I congratulate you on the capture of Malta[5] by your brave countrymen. I wanted to be the first to give you the news, but I heard that an express had been sent which would reach you long before my letter. Many events have taken place since you left us. The happy return of the Emperor, and the prolongation of the truce, among others, afford me much pleasure, although the yielding up of three fortresses, by which it was purchased, is a great drawback to our joy; but I prefer anything to war. You doubtless know that Thugut resigned ten days ago, and that his resignation was accepted; his successor, however, has not been appointed, and no official information having as yet been given, we are uncertain as to what will take place. I am in hopes that my brother will leave Palermo tomorrow, though I know nothing certain on that point, for, since the arrival of the courier who brought the news of the accouchement of the Hereditary Princess,[6] I have had no letters. Our dear and adorable Queen[7] has been very much engaged during the last few days. I believe her daughters, together with the Grand Duke,[8] sang an opera yesterday to welcome the Emperor; and to-day all the Imperial and Neapolitan family dine at Laxenburg.[9] The Queen goes sometimes to the theatre, but not often. I do not think they will leave Schönbrunn till after St.Theresa's day.[10] I confess to you that I do not think our dear Queen is looking well; perhaps my affection for her makes me more anxious than others. I should like to see her always perfectly happy and well, and would, if it were in my power, render her immortal; she well deserves to be so. As for interesting news, my dear friend, I have none to give you, but I could not resist the temptation of recalling myself to your remembrance, and wishing you fine weather and health to continue your journey. May your arrival in England be speedy and happy ! I cherish also the flattering hope of seeing you here again in the spring.[11] In the mean time think sometimes of me, dear amiable lady, and ever rely on the gratitude and tender attachment of your affectionate friend - Princess Esterházy.- My compliments, if you please, to Miss Knight,[12] and a thousand endearments to the Knight and to Mylord.")

In the middle of October, 1800, Maria Carolina too answered a letter which she had received from Lady Hamilton, probably through the same mediator. Palumbo ("Maria Carolina", pp.215 et. seq.), published the original French version of this letter from the manuscript in the British Museum (vol.1616, fol. 121, Bibl.Egerton MS.) copying the faulty orthography. We also quote again Pettigrew's translation ("Nelson", 1.398 et. seq.).

> *Schönbrunn ce 17 Octobre.- Ma chere Miledy voyez la premiere lettre que par un courier je vous ecris depuis votre depart j'ai recue une lettre de vous de Prague par Mr. Robeninchi je sais que vous avez ete en Saxe mais je n'ai point recue de vos lettres j'espere et desire que cette lettre vous trouve heurreusement arrive en Angleterre que le Chevalier soit arrive en bonne sante notre vertueux heros Nelson y soit estime cheri connu aclame come son caractere et grande actions meritent .. le jour de votre depart de Vienne et de notre separation a ete fatal pour moi c'est celui du retour de L'Empereur avec cette fatalisme honteuse armistice signe Aussy le mauvais augure de votre depart qui m'a ete si sensible a influe aussy dans les Evenement tristes ... Adieu ma chere Miledy Saluez le chevalier mon heros Nelson en mon nom et croyez moi de loin de pres et pour la vie votre reconnaissante amie - Charlotte.*

("Schönbrunn, October 17th [1800]. My dear Lady - This letter which I send you by a courier is the first I have written since your departure. I received a letter from you from Prague, by Madame Rumbeke.[13] I am aware that you have been in Saxony, but have received no letters from you during your stay there. I hope and trust that this will find you safely arrived in England and the Chevalier

*Merton Place in Surrey, the English seat of Lord Nelson. He lived here, albeit intermittently, together with the Hamiltons, and with Emma after Sir William's death up to the time of Trafalgar.*

also, and both in good health - and that our valorous hero Nelson may be esteemed, cherished, known and applauded, as his character and great actions deserve ... the day of your departure from Vienna was fatal for me, for the Emperor on that day returned with that most disgraceful armistice, signed; thus your departure which afflicted me, was also the precursor of most unfortunate events ... Adieu, my dear Lady, salute the Chevalier and my hero Nelson in my name, and believe me, whether near or distant, your grateful friend for life Charlotte.")

On November 29th, Maria Carolina had a Requiem Mass held in the *Kapuzinerkirche*, in the crypt of which lie the remains of the Habsburg family, in memory of her mother, the Empress Maria Theresa. Because of the menace of the French marching into Vienna,[14] the Court planned to move to Ofen or Brünn at the end of year.[15] Earlier, however, we find Maria Carolina with her children, together with the Emperor and Empress, the Grand Duke of Tuscany

*(a) Lady Hamilton at Merton Place. Pencil drawing by Thomas Baxter. This is the only portrait which reveals to us Emma Hamilton's features in later years.*

*(b) Horatia, Nelson's daughter, at her father's grave. Painting by W Owen.*

139

with his wife, the Archduke Anton, the Duke Albert of Sachsen-Teschen and the Palatin (Governor of Hungary) Archduke Joseph with his wife, in Eisenstadt, as guests of the Esterházys. On December 12th and 13th two Masses by Haydn were performed there in honour of the Court; one of which might have been the so-called "Nelson Mass". It is possible that this was the occasion on which Maria Carolina suggested to the master this name, for his mass.

On January 1st, 1801, Nelson was promoted Vice-Admiral, and a fortnight later he separated from his wife; there was, however, no formal divorce.[16] On January 29th Lady Hamilton gave birth to a daughter who was later to be named Horatia Nelson.

Maria Carolina's political sympathies were no longer with England as she hoped to gain more by turning towards Russia. In spite of this she was surprised and disappointed when, at the end of 1801, like other Peers, Nelson spoke in Parliament on the future of Malta against the interest of Naples. On July 28th the Queen had left the Schönbrunn castle and returned to her husband in Naples where she arrived on August 17th.

On March 22nd Lord Minto wrote to his wife from London:[17] "I went to Lord Nelson's [Merton in Surrey] on Saturday to dinner, and returned today in the forenoon ... She [Lady Hamilton] looks ultimately to the chance of marriage, as Sir W. will not be long in her way, and she probably indulges a hope that she may survive Lady Nelson; in the meanwhile she and Sir William and the whole set of them are living with him [Nelson] at his expense ... The whole house ... [is] covered with nothing but pictures of her and him... ."

Sir William Hamilton died in London on April 6th 1803 and was buried, next to his first wife in the church-yard of Milford Haven, Pembrokeshire,[18] in accordance with a vow he made. Nelson and Emma now lived in Merton together.[19] Soon after the death of Hamilton Nelson sailed to Naples on the "Victory" and arrived there simultaneously with the new Ambassador, Sir Hugh Elliot. Nelson was then Commander-in-Chief of the British Mediterranean Fleet, a post he held from 1803 till 1805. His relations with Maria Carolina by that time were not very cordial, but that did not prevent him in a letter to the Queen, on June 10th 1803, from suggesting that the pension which was intended for Lady Hamilton in the Vienna days would now be welcome.[20] Count Zinzendorf makes a note in his diary on May 7th 1805, employing a mixture of French and German:

> Ath.Z. gelesen 120 u. 131. Lady Hamilton - 1782 Miss Harte - cette fille facile, que M. Hamilton epousa, depuis que nous avons vu ici avec lui et l'amiral Nelson entschädigt ihren Mann nicht für diesen Verlust.

("Read Ath.Z. 120 and 131.[21] Lady Hamilton - 1782 Miss Harte - this damsel of easy virtue whom M.Hamilton married, after what we saw here with him and Admiral Nelson, she does not compensate her husband for this loss.")

On October 21st Nelson was killed at Trafalgar. Johann Baptist Wanhall, the composer of the *Grosse See-Schlacht bei Abukir*, dedicated another Piano work to the hero: *Die See-Schlacht bei Trafalgar und Tod des Admirals Nelson*. ("The Naval Battle of Trafalgar and Death of Admiral Nelson").[22] In the autumn of 1806 Artaria of Vienna published a *Nelson Trauermarsch* ("Nelson Funeral March") for Piano by Joseph Drechsler, who later composed the music to Ferdinand Raimund's fairy play *Der Bauer als Millionär oder Das Mädchen aus der Feenwelt* ("The Farmer as Millionaire or The Girl from Fairyland"), containing the famous duet *Brüderlein fein*. No copy of this march is now to be found.

Sometime in the middle of February 1806 Albert Christoph Dies, landscape painter and author, paid his 17th visit to Haydn, in order to collect material for his *Biographische Nachrichten von Joseph Haydn*, published in Vienna in 1810, after the master's death, as was Griesinger's work *Biographische Notizen*. In his book, Dies on February 19th (p.112) describes the visit:

> *Es schien ihn besonders zu vergnügen, dass ich ein paar Worte über sein Klavier gesagt, er fand den Einfall komisch, dass ich es einen "unzahlbaren Schatz" genannt, und den Liebhabern von Seltenheiten einen so zweideutigen Wink gegeben hatte. Bot man doch, sagte ich, dem Wundarzt, der die Kugel besitzt, die Nelson tötete, für den elenden Bleiklumpen schon 100 Guineen; nun wird doch ihr schöpferisches Klavier so viel wert sein, als jene vernichtende Kugel? - "In London", sagte Haydn, "hat man Sinn für so Etwas! Ich sah wirklich Händel's Klavier bei dem Könige, der es der Familie abkaufte und als eine Reliquie aufbewahrt."*

("It seemed to amuse him especially that I said a few words about his piano;[23] he thought the idea funny, that I called it a 'priceless treasure', and had thus given such an ambiguous hint to lovers of rarities. 'The surgeon who owns the bullet which killed Nelson',[24] I said, 'was offered 100 guineas for the miserable lump of lead; surely your creative piano is as valuable as that destructive bullet?' - 'In London', said Haydn, 'such things are appreciated! I actually saw Handel's piano which the King bought from the family and keeps as a relic'."[25])

At that time the Queen of England presented Haydn with a copy of Handel's German Oratorio: *Der für die Sünden der Welt gemarterte und sterbende Jesus* (1716), which Haydn later intended to leave to the publishing firm of Breitkopf & Härtel.

Haydn died in Vienna in 1809, during the second French occupation of the city. In Sauer's catalogue of the master's art treasures[26] which were sold by auction on March 26th 1810, we find the following: Lot *No.8: Admiral Nelson von Neidl* (Admiral Nelson by Neidl), *No.9: ditto, ein anderes* (ditto, another), described as copper plates in a portfolio, and *No.29: Plan der Schlacht von Abukir, englisch* (Plan of the Battle of Aboukir, English); probably Vivares' engraving.[27] The two portraits, valued by Sauer 10 Kreuzer the pair, were sold for 12 Kreuzer, the battle picture, valued 60 Kreuzer, was sold for 1 florin and 30 Kreuzer. Lot No. 358 is described: *Nelson Missa in D minor/ geschrieben in Eisenstadt 1798, eigenhändige Partitur*, ("Nelson Mass in D minor / written in Eisenstadt in 1798, autograph score"). We can see from this that the Mass was then definitely named after Nelson, and we have shown earlier in the book that it received this title before Haydn's death. It is not known how this manuscript came to the Vienna *Hofbibliothek*, and it is surprising that it was not among the rest of the musical works left by Haydn, which went en bloc to Eisenstadt. It is possible that the Esterházy family gave it to the *Hofbibliothek* in 1820, a small recompense for Vienna when Haydn's body was removed to Eisenstadt.

On November 28th 1811 the Viennese authoress Karolina Pichler sent a number of autographs to Goethe in Weimar for his collection, including one of Nelson and one of Haydn; Goethe thanked her for them on March 31st 1812.[28] Unfortunately we do not know the nature of those autographs; the one of Nelson is probably connected with his stay in Vienna. The autographs sent to Goethe, apparently all of them letters, belonged to Mrs.Eleonore Fliess, née Eskeles, of Vienna. Eleonore, on whose behalf Karolina Pichler sent them, met Goethe when he was taking the waters at Carlsbad. When she died on 20th August 1812, the poet wrote to her sister-in-law, Cäcilie von Eskeles, on November 26th 1812, mourning their common loss. So it is likely that the letters of Nelson and Haydn, which were given to Goethe, had been written either to Mrs.von Eskeles or to Mrs.von Arnstein.

In 1813, Maria Carolina fled from her tormentor, Lord William Bentinck,[29] and retired to the Hetzendorf castle near Schönbrunn, where she died seven months later on September 8th. Her granddaughter, Marie Louise, the wife of Napoleon, then exiled on Elba, was living there at the time. Maria Carolina of Naples was buried in the Capucin Vault, Vienna, near her mother.

Lady Hamilton died in Calais, on January 15th 1815, quite destitute. Lady Nelson who had become blind, survived the three friends of her hero husband.

The memory of Nelson and Lady Hamilton soon paled in Austria and Hungary after their visit, but the two months in Austria and Hungary (from August 1st to October 1st 1800) and especially the forty days in and around Vienna - "an uninterrupted festival", as Dumas[30] called it - remained a beautiful memory for the English friends. As an episode of interest in the life of Britain's greatest sailor, and thus in the annals of Britain's glorious history, it was thought worth while to throw full light on these sixty eventful days.

## Postscript.

In the auction of Haydn's estate there was also a living creature. The last Lot, no.614, of his "art treasures" is described in the auction catalogue as : *Ein lebendiger Papagei aus dem Geschlechte der gelehrigen Jako's in Taubengrösse, grau mit rotem Schweif. Da die Papageis nach allen Naturhistorikern ein hohes Alter bei 100 Jahren erleben, so ist dieser noch jung. Herr Haydn kaufte denselben vor 19 Jahren, noch nicht völlig erwachsen. in London um einen hohen Preis, und unterrichtete ihn selbst. Wohnt, wie gewöhnlich, in einem blechernen Hause.*

("A live parrot of the teachable Jaco species[31] about the size of a dove, grey with a red tail. Since, according to all natural historians, parrots live to an advanced age of as much as 100 years, this one may be said to be still young. Herr Haydn bought it 19 years ago, for a high price in London, when it was still not yet fully grown, and trained it himself. Living, as usual, in a metal cage.")

It is known from the biographers of Haydn that this parrot lived in the master's suburban house in Vienna. In warm weather it stood in its cage in the courtyard and mockingly imitated the sparrows on the neighbouring roofs. But it could also whistle an entire octave or call to its master: "Come Papa Haydn to the beautiful Pollykins!". It could also whistle the beginning of the Austrian people's hymn which, towards the end of his life, "Papa" Haydn played on his piano every day. Thus the parrot, whose value had been estimated at 100 Gulden, actually realized 1415 Gulden, at which price it was bought by Prince Johann Josef Liechtenstein[32]. (His brother-in-law, Esterházy, had had to pay only 4500 Gulden for the whole of the music left by Haydn.) Nothing is known of the further history of this *rara avis*. The sequel may be that the parrot is still alive, for this would entail an age of about 150 years by no means a severe burden for so long-lived a bird to support. In that event there is, still in existence, a solitary witness of the encounter between Haydn and Nelson, and, if the bird could be found, having grown so much cleverer in the interval, it could surely tell us more of that meeting than, in the absence of such evidence, has been vouchsafed to the present author's investigations. O.E.D. (1946).

1 T.A. Evans, "A Statement of the Means by which the Nelson Coat... was obtained...Together with copies of letters ... relating to Lord Nelson and Lady Hamilton, now in the possession of the Editor...", London 1846, pp.28-30.

2 Evans read: de Rombeh.

3 Evans read: Hobeners. Cf. Palumbo's "Robeninchi" in the following letter by Maria Carolina.

4 The brother of Princess Maria Josefa Hermenegild Esterházy, nee Liechtenstein, was apparently Johann Josef Prince Liechtenstein, the Austrian Field Marshal, who in 1805 succeeded his elder brother, Alois Josef, to the throne of Liechtenstein. Her youngest brother, Philipp Josef, was also an officer.

5 5th September.

6 Archduchess Clementine, wife of Franz, the Crown Prince of Naples.

7 The Queen of Naples.

8 The Grand Duke of Tuscany.

9 Another summer residence of the Habsburgs, south of Vienna.

10 15th October.

11 Lady Hamilton never returned to Austria.

12 Evans read : Reay.

13 Palumbo prints "Robeninchi", Pettigrew "Robemirchi".

14 After General Moreau had defeated the Austrians again on December 3rd at Hohenlinden, before the last armistice (at Steyr), which was followed by the Peace of Luneville, at the beginning of 1801.

15 This never took place.

16 A divorce would have been possible only by a Private Act of Parliament.

17 "Life and Letters of ... Minto", 111.242.

18 As a memorial to Nelson, the second Lady Hamilton placed in the church of Milford Haven the truck of *L'Orient*, Greville, Hamilton's heir, died in Pembrokeshire in 1807.

19 "Dispatches and Letters of ... Nelson", V.84.

20 Her second child, named Emma, only lived from February until August 1804.

21 It is not certain if the reading of the Athens newspapers had anything to do with this unintelligible note.

22 The only copy known to exist is in the *Preussische Staatsbibliothek*, Berlin. It has the French title *Le Combat navale de Trafalgar et la Mort de Nelson*, published by the Berlin *Bureau de Musique*.

23 This refers to a remark made by Dies in his 15th visit on January 14th 1806 (Dies, *Nachrichten*, p. 97).

24 Sir William Beatty, the surgeon of the "Victory", who edited the "Authentic narrative of the death of Lord Nelson", London 1807. The bullet was never sold but went into the possession of the Royal Family.

25 The harpsichord made by Hans Ruckers the Elder, dated 1612, now in Windsor Castle.

26 *Archiv der Stadt Wien*; a copy is in the *Nationalbibliothek*, Vienna.

27 It was possibly a gift of Nelson's to Haydn. The British Museum possesses several scenes of this battle (see "Catalogue of the Printed Maps, Plans, and Charts", London 1885, p[.2994) & Suppl. 1906). There are more such prints in the National Maritime Museum.

28 Cf. Karoline Pichler's *Denkwürdigkeiten meines Lebens*, Munich 1914,1.392 and 628; August Sauer *Goethe und Österreich*, Weimar 1904, 11.256 and 271; and Gustav Gugitz: *Zu einer Briefstelle Mozarts* in *Mozarteum-Mitteilungen*, Salzburg 1921,111,2-3.

29 He had served under the Archduke Charles in 1800/1, and before that under General Suvorov. In 1811 he was British Ambassador and Commander in Palermo, and from 1812 to 1814 Commander-in-Chief of Sicily.

30 Alexander Dumas père: *Emma Lyonna*, a historical novel, Paris 1876; translated by Hervey L.Williams, London [1903].

31 In G.L.L. Comte de Buffon's *Histoire naturelle des oiseaux*, Paris 1779, vol.Vi, pp. 100 et. seq., *Le Jaco ou Perroquet cendré* is described, and the coloured plate 311 of the portfolio of engravings by François Nicolas Martinet of 1787 portrays charmingly *Le Jaco ou Perroquet cendré de Guinée*.

32 Dickens' stuffed raven was sold at Christie's, a month after the poet's death, with his other relics, for £126.

# *Appendices*

## HAMMER'S GERMAN POEM ON ABOUKIR[1]

Auf Den Sieg der Britten vor Alexandria

- minuit furorem
Vix una sospes navis ab ignibus
Mentemque lympherum Mareotico
Redegit in veros timores
*Nelson* ab Italia volantem
Remis adurgens.
                    Hor:

Gebieterin der Meere, Britannia!
Auf Fluten tronend, Freiin am Themsestrand,
        Sultanin an des Ganges Ufern,
        Horche dem Wogengetüm der Wasser!

Das heilige Vorgebirg *Lusitaniens*[2]
Der *Nordsee* Brandung, Afrika's Vorgebirg
        Der Hoffnung, nun der Nil mit sieben
        Zungen erbrausen von deinem Ruhme.

Wo Philipp's Sohn, der Welteroberer,
Den Fluten einen Hafen entsteigen liess;
        (Er dachte nicht, dass einst nach Jahren
        Zweier zermalmender Republiken

Gepries'ne Heeresführer bei traurigen
Gestirnen hier nach schimmerndem Tatenlauf
        Zu Todeshekatombe landen
        Würden, *Pompejus* und *Buonaparte*!)

Wo einst Egypten's Kiele, entfliehend den
*Liburnen*,[3] heimwärts eilend von Actium,
        Im Angesicht der Burg des stolzen
        Weibes mit Mast und mit Mann versanken:

Dort tilgt mit feuer *Nelson Duilius*
Das Flottenheer des Feind's, der - berauschet von
    Des Glückes Becher - tief verwöhnt ist,
    Alles zu hoffen, und nichts zu fürchten.

Der Pharos von dem Port Alexander's ist
Erloschen, die Paläste Kleopatra's
    Sind Trümmer, längst mit Schilf verwachsen;
    Selbst Pyramiden zerstieben einstens.

Seht Völker! Die gigantische Flotte flammt,
Ein Pharos, leuchtend vor dem Palaste, den
    Britannia, die Meeresgöttin,
    Über den Ozean sich erbaut hat;

Und *Nelson's* Name pranget als Giebelstein
Der höchsten Pyramide des Schlachtenruhms,
    Auf deren Stufen *Howe* und *Dunkan*,
    *Jervis* und *Elfinstone* sich erheben.

Josef von Hammer

## HÖDL'S LATIN POEM ON ABOUKIR[4]

Nelsonis
Anglicani Belliducis Victoria
Navali Pugna ad Nili Fluminis Ostia
Calendio Augusti Anni MDCCXCVIII
Reportata
lnclytae Nationis Anglicanae
Honoribus
Ab Ebreichsdorfensi Musa Festivo Elego
Decantata


Sopronii Typis Annae Clarae Siess.


In
Belliducem Buonaparte
Spe tumida et velis orientem quaeris: at erras,
Occasum invenies, Dux Bonaparte tuum.

*146*

In

Belliducem Nelson

Laeva tibi manus est, sublata est dextera: fors proin,
Haud mirarer ego, si tibi laeva foret;
Sed quoniam dextre pugnasti, laurea serta,
Victoris retulit praemia, laeva manus.

Gallia! siste tuos plausus, gemitusque resume!
Alea versa: micant fata sinistra tibi:
Abjice jam lauros, tragicam tibi sume cupressum!
Illis deciduis, convenit ista tibi.
Pugnatum pelago est: ovat Anglica classis et ora
Nili Gallorum sanguine tincta fluunt.
Aegyptus, quo migrasti, nova laurea serta
Ut legeres, Thule est ultima facta tibi,
Jussa ubi tu fueras victricem sistere cursum
Extremas fati mox subitura vices.

Nelsonis superae virtuti victima tandem
Cessisti: Heu! classis tota subacta tua est;
Flos potior Martis, tua gloria, millia plura,
Erecta Anglorum succubuere manu.
Pars ratium consumta foco, pars aequore mersa,
Vix ternis datus est trasitus effugio;
Pars major facta est spolium, aeductaque in Urbem[5]
Plaudentis populi conspicienda oculis.
Gallia! siste tuos plausus, gemitusque resume!
Alea versa: micant fata sinistra tibi.

Russia, quae dudum siluit, pacemque colebat,
Arma movet, turmis ingruit illa suis,
Exitiumque tibi terra pelagoque minatur,
Extremum, solido Marte, opibusque potens.
Quid, quod Luna etiam, fuerat que semper amico
Foedere juncta tibi, te modo persequitur?
Publico et edicto, verbisque tonantibus, ira
Frendens, indicit martia signa tibi;
Sunt patulae factae, quas volvis pectore, fraudes,
Noscere perfidias incipit illa tuas.

Hinc te, cui gentem fallacem jussit ab oris
Emigrare suis, est inimica tibi.
Jam tuus in septem conclusus turribus haeret
Legatus, rigido carcere triste gemens.

Gallia, siste tuos plausus, gemitusque resume!
Alea versa: micant fata sinistra tibi.

Incassum tibi blandiris spe vana et inani:
Anglorum Hibernos nolle subesse jugo.
Sunt motus jam compositi, quos foverat ante
Turba rebellantum, seque dedere Throno,
Anglorumque manus dominas proni venerantur,
Haudque tuum proscunt amplius auxilium;
Incassum tentas illuc deducere classim,
Vix portum attingent agmina, vincta gement.
Gallia! siste tuos plausus, gemitusque resume!
Alea versa: micant fata sinistra tibi.

Sortem plange tuam tu comprimis, Bonaparte,
Fortuna ac Anglis flebile ludibrium
Desine praeteritos posthac numerare triumphos,
Desine in elato plaudere porro sinu!
Classe tua eversa quid ages jam, Dux miserande?
Orbatus tanto milite, tot ratibus?
Qui poteris modo prosequi iter, qui praelia ferre,
Qui lauros victor continuare tuas?

Numquid grex Arabum per te devictus, in ermem
Cum te Mavortis robore conspicient,
Jungent sese Anglis, armisque animusque resumtis,
Tecum iterum cupient conseruisse manus?
Nec pugnis ponent finem, dum denique fracto
Deficiant miles sensim, animique tibi,

Victusque evadas spolium subeasque catenas
Barbaricae gentis lugubre mancipium,
Dicaturque: Amplis nuper qui scribere leges
Visus erat Regnis, Heu! modo vincla gerit.
Belliducem infaustum! plango tua fata: - Miselle!
Hunc tandem finem gloria nacta tua est.


Haec igitur clades tua fit, Bonapartem magistra:
Fortunae dubias noscere disce vices;
Est falla, est inconstans: ne crede micanti,
Cui blanda est hodie, cras nocet illa iterum.-
Ne tamen heroes animos hic sortis acerbae

Impetus infringat, ejiciatque tuos.
Virtute obfirma mentem, pectusque supremo
Robore, fallacis despice tela Deae.
Ingenio polles, ac ausibus: ultima tenta,
Hostium ut eludas effugiendo manus.

Fors nummis redimi dabitur? - - medio utere eodem,
Palmas ausonias quo tibi nactus eras:
Victores corrumpe tuos fulgente metallo,
Auro ac argento vincula deme tibi!- -
At vereor: nihil efficies hac arte, dolore
Tu simili haud Turcas fascinat iste nitor.
Nec quidquam evincet tua Proclamatio, qua tu
Legem Ottomanam, ceu sacra jura probas.
Sacrilego cultu Mahometem devenerando;
Haud credet dictis Natio cauta tuis.

Id te soletur, dum portes vincula, cladis
Culpa quod exactae haud fit tribuenda tibi.
Absens turn recte fueras: terrestria miscens
Praelia cum oppositis, gente feroce, Begis.
Fors classis tua, te praesente, haud passa fuisset
Hanc stragem, semper tu Vigil Argus eras.
Hinc si fata darent etiam te compede stringi,
Magnanimi titulus te manet usque Ducis, - -

Gallia!  Culpa tua est haec clades, Tu renuenti
Hoc iter ut faceret, jussa Duci dederas:
Incauto in consilio, temerario et ausu
Susceptisti opus hoc tanta pericla viae,
Fortuitasque vices, tot belli obstacula, porto
Ac Terra turmis insuperanda tuis.
Per te, Rectoresque tuos Dux inclytus iste.
Heu! cedet Turcis triste sacrificium.
Culpa tua est, tot turmarum, ratiumque ruina,
Culpa tua est classis totius excidium.

Edic: quid tibi jam superest? — Tandem resipisce,
Atque tui fastus pone supercilium!
Jam gressus moderare tuos tumidiumque volatum
Noli Daedaleo jungere te Puero.
Est casus nimium durus, qui venit ab alto,
Deciduum feriunt vulnera plura caput.

Accisae tibi nunc alae, collisaque crura:
Cum Bonaparte tuo, spes cecidere tuae.
Neve tuam posthac Thetidi committito fortem
Est ea amica Anglis, est inimica tibi.
Quin aequis potius pacem componito pactis,
Si sapis, hoc nostro nitere consilio.

Tu vero florens Regnum Anglia! plaude, triumpha!
Da, possim laudes vota que ferre tibi:
Syrtis ut in pelago, tumidis, agitata procellis,
Inviolata tamen fluctibus usque manet,
Sic tua permansit victrix Constantia, ridens
Gallorum motus, terrificasque minas.
Sunt tanti tituli, fulgentia tot monumenta,
Tot tua facta, quibus condecorata nites,
Te merito ut Matrem Heroum, Dominamque tumentis
Compellem pelagi, cui mario unda subest,
Cujus navalem virtutem cultior orbis,
Et stupet, et celebrat, laurigeramque vocat.

Iamque tui in gremio Regni decerne trophaeum
Nelsoni invictum glorificando Ducem!
Fac: rutilans surgat Syrio de marmore moles,
Magnanimo dignum construe pegma Duci.
Sint lauri circumpositae myrthique, colossi
Erecti postes florida serta tegant.
Roma suis ut caesaribus formare solebat
Olim, sic nitidis fulgeat ille notis,
Ac una exuviis prostrato de hoste relatis,
Scilicet ereptis ensibus, ac galcis,
Confrāctis ratium tabulis, velisque rescissis,
Nec desint Statuae, nec simulacra operi.
Haec Ducis enarrent invicti grandia facta,
Quorum nunc testes Nilus et aequor erant.

E medio emineat fulgens Nelsonis imago,
Terifico Gallis ore vibrando minas.
Vulnus cui inflictum blando medicamine sanes
Hygeia, incalumem porro valere jubeus
Neptunus dextrum latus occupet, atque sinistrum
Mavors, laureolam nectat uterque Duci
Cingendo supero plausu, laudesque canendo
Tempora Victoris, talia verba ciens:

"Tu laurum, Te laurus amat, tua gloria laurus
Semper erat laurum tradimus ambo tibi,
Una supremum Te proclamando Ministrum,
Cui posthac subsint flumina et unda maris.
Quo tu cunque tuam cupies deducere classim,
Semper ei nostro Numine proni erimus."
Adque basim molis constructae stet Bonaparte
Nelsonem aspiciens, hos repetendo tonos:
"Jam lauros Tibi cedo meas: mea gloria posthac
Sit tua, Victorem Te colo, Te veneror.
Tutelae me trado tuae, defende misellum!
Ne fors barbaricum cogar adire jugum."

Laurigera haec moles siet eo usque erecta, notetque
Palmas Nelsonis, dum patriam is repetat,
lpseque tum videat structa hac in imagine: Quanti
Anglia Belliducem grata suum appretiet.

| | |
|---|---|
| Cecini | Joachimus Hödl |
| Ebreichsdorfii in Austria | Parochus jubilatus |
| inferiori ad limites | oppidi Werschetz in |
| Hungariae | Banatu |

## MISS KNIGHT'S ENGLISH POEM ON ABOUKIR[6]

The
Battle of the Nile
A Pindarick Ode


To His Excellency
The R$^t$.Honb$^{le}$.
Sir William Hamilton,
K.B. His Britannick Majesty's
Minister Plenipotentiary and Envoy Extraordinary
At the Court of the Two Sicilies

etc.etc.etc.

Vienna,
Printed by Widow Alberti
1800.

Sir,

It was your wish that I should dedicate a few lines to the celebration of the greatest action that ever adorned the splendid annals of our naval history. This motive alone would have induced me to undertake so arduous a task; though, were my abilities equal to my feelings, I should want no other impulse to sing the praises so justly due to the Hero of the Nile, and his brave associates.

However inadequate the following poem may be deemed to the glorious event it is intended to record, I take the liberty of addressing it to your Excellency, or to the friend, of Sir Horatio Nelson, as to a Minister, whose zeal and talents have always stood formost in promoting the happiness and real interest of his own country, and that in which he resides, and, permit me to add, as a tribute of gratitude from a daughter of the waves for the distinguished attentions conferred on the British navy by Sir William Hamilton and his amiable Lady

I have the honour to be,
Sir,
with the sincerest esteem
Your Excellency's obliged humble servant
Ellis Cornelia Knight.

Naples, 15. September, 1798

- 1 -

Bear me, some eagle to yon laurel grove,
Where on the topmost bough sublime
(A height no mortal can unaided climb)
The golden lyre attracts Apollo's rays,
The lyre of glory and of love,
Doom'd to record the Hero's deathless praise:
And hark! responsive to the sounding strings
Hesperia's coast with exultation rings.

- 2 -

Where late pale terror stalk'd his magick round,
And every fair and fertile plain,
Drooping beneath his pestilential reign
Each fading flowret wept,
Each lofty palm that graced the hallow'd ground, -
Where for succeeding ages peaceful slept
The sacred ashes of her Chiefs revered

By prostrate nations idolized and fear'd. -

- 3 -

Ausonia trembling 'midst unnumbered woes
Sat lost in silent grief,
Hopeless, nor daring to implore relief,
Oppress'd with present ills and dreading future harms:
She saw her base, insulting foes
Despoil her of her envied charms,
And with rapacious fury bear away
Minerva's treasure, their too beauteous prey.

- 4 -

Nor earth nor sea the baneful tempest spares;
Tyrrhenian waves receive their numerous prows,
Corrupting gold in torrents flows,
Their standard insurrection lifts on high,
Treason, alarm, mistrust their way prepares,
And far as rage impels - their banners fly;
When, lo! from Ocean's trophied mansions come
The Sons of Neptune to pronounce their doom.

- 5 -

Led by a warrior, whose intrepid soul
Pure faith and daring courage sway,
This band of brothers cuts the liquid way;
A small, determined band, their country's pride,
Whom neither arts ensnare nor threats control,
Like purest gold by fiery dangers tried;
The guilty spoiler quits his destined prize,
Shrinks from their vengeful arm, and trembling flies.

- 6 -

But vain his flight, his forced resistance vain,
Though, shelter'd by famed Egypt's flood,
Secure he deem'd his thundering bulwarks stood.
Tremendous justice in great Nelson's form
With valour, conduct in his train,
And every virtue that from freedom springs,

Calm and undaunted 'mid the rising storm
Destruction bears on her triumphant wings.

- 7 -

Since sage Sesostris ruled this fertile clime
(His car by captive Monarchs drawn),
Whom arts illumined with their roseate dawn.
Whom science dignified, and wisdom led,
Through the long lapse of time,
No scene more glorious graced old Nilus' bed;
Though Persia's Victor came yon walls to rear,
And mighty Julius fought, and conquer'd here.

- 8 -

With hope renew'd the Gallick navy rode,
Pleased to behold the Briton's thin array;
Courting the terrors of the vengeful day
She, like Busiris earth and heaven defied:
Each lofty vessel from her side
Pourd winged deaths in furious mood;
Beneath their weight deep groan'd the subject flood,
And chief where mark'd as leader of the rest
The giant Orient stood aloft confest.

- 9 -

Britannia's leader gives the dread command;
Obedient to his summons flames arise;
The fierce explosion seeks the skies,
And high in air the pond'rous mass is thrown
The dire concussion shakes the strand;
Earth, air, and sea affrighted groan;
The solid Pyramids attest the shock,
And their firm bases to the centre rock.

- 1 0 -

Roused with the sound great Philip's martial son
Arises from his honourd grave;
His piercing eye beholds the warrior brave,
And emulation in his bosom glows:

"Enough!" he cries, "thy task is done;
 "I see, I see, bold Chief, thy country's foes
"Confess thy valour, their debasement own:
"A fairer wreath thy godlike toils acquire
"Than all the crowns that graced my funeral pyre. -

- 11 -

"'Tis thine to vindicate thy country's laws
"To stem impetuous rapine's tide;
"To lop the crest of stern tyrannick pride,
"And add new trophies to thy native coast:
"Thine be the heartfelt, just applause,
"And thine of conscious worth the boast!
"Eternal praise, great Nelson! to thy name,
"And these immortal partners of thy fame!"

- 12 -

He said, when slow appeard a Latian chief
Of warlike semblance, graceful mien,
And with him Egypt's last and brightest Queen
On Albion's Hero smile the hapless pair
Forgetful of their former grief;
With cheerful notes the victor's joy they share
And thus the Roman "Conqueror receive
"A Soldier's praise": 'tis all he now can give.

- 13 -

"When Britain first withstood great Caesar's might,
"Undisciplined she scorn'd to yield;
"Our firmest legions scarce maintaind the field;
"Like young Alcides vigorous from her birth
"Now science aids her in the fight,
"And learned arts assist her inborn worth
"Victorious with expanded wings she soars,
"And rolls her thunders o'er remotest shores."

- 14 -

More had he said, but from his humble tomb
The shade of laurel'd Pompey rose,

He views the Britons victors of their foes;
The Nile with wrecks o'erspread the curling smoke.
The captive banners seal the doom
Of haughty France, and break her galling yoke.
"See! proud oppression falls". The chief exclaims
"Perish her empire 'mid these sanguine flames.

- 15 -

"Blest leader! whom thy country's voice approves,
"Whom rescued nations must adore,
"Whom I thought lost on treacherous Egypt's shore,
"Exulting greet, and in thy Paeans join!
"Each son of fame the Hero loves,
"Nor will I envious at thy deeds repine,
"Though once my name stood foremost in renown
"Of all whose brows adorn the rostral crown.

- 16 -

"O may that crown long grace thy honour'd head
"With ever blooming laurel twined,
"And oaken wreaths by sapient Heaven design'd
"The growth of Britain and to Britons due
"Who kingdoms free from servile dread;
"And thou benign, with these illustrious few
"Who share thy toils and emulate thy worth,
"Hear, these prophetick words, to which thy deeds give birth.

- 17 -

"Though vice and guilt their numerous conquest boast,
"Yet virtue has her sails unfurl'd
"To save a sinking, a deluded world;
"Her sons assert her empire o'er the main,
"Spread terror round each hostile coast,
"And teach mankind to bless her generous reign
"Britannia's palms shall break the guilty charm,
"Rouse latent valour, and bid Europe arm."

1 To page 53 of this book.

2 The foothills of St Vincent Portugal were known in ancient times as Promontorium Sacrum (Promontorium means foothills).

3 Liburne - that was the indication for light sailboats Augustus used during the successful battle at Actium/Greece on 2 Sept.31 BC against the Egyptian fleet of Marcus Antonius.

4 To page 64 of this book.

5 Londinium (London).

6 To pages 107-113 of this book.

## Nelson Music

In addition to the music discussed in this book:

Anonymous: "Nelson's Victory. A Sonata for the Piano Forte. Inscribed to his Lordship by the Author." With programmatic notes. London [1798], Longman & Broderip (Bodleian and British Museum).

J. Mathews: "Nelson & the Tars of Old England, a New Song [on] ... Sir Horatio Nelson's Victory over the French Fleet, etc." Bath [1798], the author (British Museum).

J. Moulds: "Nelson's Cap, or the Badge of Honor, etc." Song. London [1798], W.Hodsoll (British Museum).

R. Spofforth: "Nelson's Victory, a much Admired Song. Written by Mr.G. Fox." London [1798], Longman & Broderip (British Museum).

S.F. Rimbault: "The Hero of the Nile, or Nelson Victorious. A Song on that Glorious Event." London [about 1798], T. Preston (British Museum; University Library, Cambridge).

Anonymous: "Nelson & Victory, Fought off the Mouth of the Nile, 1st Augst, 1798. (With a list of the English and French Fleets.) 18 new Country Dances for 1799. Sold by the principal Haberdasher in London." -A fan, from Lady Charlotte Schreiber's Collection (British Museum, Department of Prints).

T. Attwood: "The Mouth of the Nile, a ... Musical Entertainment in Honor of the Glorious first of August ... The Words by T. Dibdin." London [1799], Goulding, Phipps & D'Almaine (British Museum).

C.Burney: [No title.] A popular song on the naval victories, the five naval British heroes of the present war, the words also by Burney, produced at Covent

Garden in 1799, but never printed; the manuscript apparently lost. (See Burney's "Memoirs", London 1832, vol. 3, pp. 268-270).

J.Mazzinghi: "Admiral Lord Nelson's Victory. A Sonata for the Piano Forte. In Commemoration of the Glorious 1st of August, 1798." London [1798], Goulding, Phipps & D'Almaine (Admiralty Library and British Museum).

D.Corri: "Nelson's Victory. A Characteristic Sonata, with Tamburino Accompaniment, Expressly Composed & dedicated to Baron Nelson ... In Honour of the ever Memorable 1st of August 1798." With programmatic note on the titlepage. London [about 1799], Corri, Dussek & Co. (Paul Hirsch Library, Cambridge).

C.G. Ferrari: "A Favourit Cantata for Voice and Chorus, dedicated to Lord Nelson". (The titlepage is decorated with an engraving: The Pyramids and a ship blowing up at sea). - No copy known.

C. Dibdin: "Nelson and the Navy" (Song, words by the composer, used in his Table Entertainment "A Tour to the Land's End"). London [1800], the Author (British Museum).

Anonymous: "Battle of the Nile" (Song) - p.6 of vol.1 of "The Gentlemen's Vade Mecum, or Pocket Companion for the German Flute." London [about 1804], H.Andrews (Rowe Library, King's College, Cambridge). this song became very popular in the United States of America.

M.P.King and J.Braham: "A Melo-Dramatic Piece, being an occasional attempt to commemorate The Death and Victory of Lord Viscount Nelson. Written by R.Cumberland". Performed at Drury Lane on Nov. 11, 1805. Libretto. London [1805], Luke Hansard (National Library of Scotland, Edinburgh). Of the music, only the song "Nelson" by Braham, later inserted in the comic opera "The Americans" (words by S.J. Arnold, music by King and Braham, 1811) was printed as "The Death of Nelson", also called "The Victory and Death of Lord Viscount Nelson" (a copy of D. Corri's edition in the University Library, Cambridge), and used, e.g. by Ferdinand Ries, as theme of variations.

G.Lanza, Junior: "Britannia Weeps, A Funeral Monody on ... Viscount Nelson, written by Mr. Orme" (with Nelson's portrait on the titlepage). Song. London [1805], Goulding, Phipps, D'Almaine & Co. (King's Music Library, British Museum).

W. Shield: "Sons of Britannia triumphant shall mourn". Song. - No copy known.

J. Watlen: "The Glorious Battle of Trafalgar". Descriptive music with vocal conclusion. - No copy known.

Anonymous: In "The Gentleman's Amusement ... for the Flute, Violin & Patent Flageolet." London [about 1810], J. Balls (Rowe Library, King's College, Cambridge):

"Lord Nelson's March" - vol.1, p.30;
"Lady Hamilton's Waltz" - vol.2, p. 17;
"Lord Nelson's Hornpipe" - vol.2, p.20;
"Lord Nelson's Waltz" - vol.2, p.22;
"King of Naples Hornpipe" - vol.2, p.31;
"God save the Emperor" (Haydn's Austrian Hymn) - vol.3, p.23.

# Bibliography

Abafi, Ludwig: *Geschichte der Freimaurerei in Österreich-Ungarn*, Vienna 1890ff.

Anon., (Edward Berry): *An authentic Narrative...of the glorious Battle of the Nile*, London 1798

Anon.: *Charles van Schorel de Wilryck ou le Fualdès Belge*, London 1826.

Arneth, Alfred, Ritter von (Ed): *Briefe der Kaiserin Maria Theresia an ihre Kinder und Freunde*, Vienna 1821

Brand, Carl Maria: *Die Messen von Joseph Haydn*, Würzburg 1941

Burney, Charles: *The present State of Music in Germany* .... London 2/1775

Corbett-Smith, A.: *Nelson,* London 1926

Curiel, Carl L.: *Il teatro San Pietro di Trieste 1690-1801*, Milan 1937

Damas, Roger de: *Memoires*, Paris 1917

Dies, Albert Christoph: *Biographische Nachrichten von Joseph Haydn*, Vienna 1810

Gamlin, Hilda: *Nelson's Friendships*, London 1899

Griesinger, Georg August: *Biographische Notizen über Joseph Haydn*, Leipzig 1810

Hanslick, Eduard: *Geschichte des Concertwesens in Wien*, Vienna 1869

Harrison, James: *The Life of the Right Honourable Horatio Lord Viscount Nelson*, London 1806

Helfert, Alexander Freiherr von: *Zeugenverhör über Maria Carolina... aus der Zeit vor der grossen französischen Revolution*, Vienna 1879

Idem: *Königin Karoline von Neapel und Sicilien im Kampf gegen die französische Weltherrschaft 1790 bis 1814*, Vienna 1878

Idem: *Maria Karolina von Österreich ... Anklagen und Verteidigung*, Vienna 1884

Keesbacher, Fr.: *Die Philharmonische Gesellschaft in Laibach*, Leipzig 1862

Kelly, Michael: *Reminiscences*, London 1826

Knight, Ellis Cornelia: *Autobiography*, London 1861

Lewis, Ludwig: *Geschichte der Freimaurerei in Österreich*, Vienna 1861

Mahan, A. T: *The Life of Nelson*, London 2/1899

Malmesbury, Third Earl of (Ed): *Series of Letters of the First Earl of Malmesbury*, London 1870

Melville, Lewis: *The Life and Letters of William Beckford of Fonthill*, London 1910

Minto, Countess (Nina) of (Ed): *Life and Letters of Sir Gilbert Elliot, First Earl of Minto, from 1751 to 1806*, London 1874

Nicolas, N. Harris (Ed): *The Dispatches and Letters of Vice-Admiral Lord Viscount Nelson*, London 1845

Paget, August B. (Ed): *The Paget Papers* .... London 1896

Pichler, Karoline, *Denkwürdigkeiten meines Lebens*, Munich 1914

Pettigrew, Thomas Joseph: *Memoirs of the Life of Vice-Admiral Lord Viscount Nelson*, London 1849

Pohl, C. F. - Botstiber, Hugo: *Joseph Haydn*, Berlin 1875/1927 and 1928

Pohl, C. F.: *Mozart und Haydn in London*, Vienna 1867

Redding, Cyrus (Ed): *Memoirs of Beckford (Dreams, Waking Thoughts and Incidents)*, London 1895

Sauer, August: *Goethe und Österreich*, Weimar 1904

Schlosser, Julius: *Geschichte der Portraitbildnerei in Wachs, Jahrbuch der kunsthistorischen Sammlungen*, Vienna 1911

Schurig, Arthur: *Leopold Mozarts Reiseaufzeichnungen*, Leipzig 1920

Sichel, Walter: *Emma Lady Hamilton*, London 3/1907

Stöger, J.N.: *Scriptores Austriacae Societatis Jesu*, Vienna 1856

Trench, R.C. (Ed): *Remains* (Melesina St. George, Journal kept during a visit to Germany in 1799, 1800)

Varnhagen van Ense, K.A.: *Vermischte Schriften*, Leipzig 2/1843

Vivenot, Alfred von: *Vertrauliche Briefe des Freiherrn von Thugut*, Vienna 1872

Wurzbach, C.v.: *Biographisches Lexikon des Kaisertums Österreich*, Vienna 1863

## Source of Illustrations
Archive of Otto Erich Deutsch: 18, 23, 43, 73, 131
Archive of the *Gesellschaft der Musikfreunde* (Austrian Society of Music Lovers): 49
*Museum der Stadt Wien* (Vienna City Museum): 53
Musical collection of the *Nationalbibliothek* (Austrian National Library): 63, 100, 109
Musical collection of the *Wiener Stadtbibliothek* (Vienna City Library): 52
National Museum, Budapest: 99
National Portrait Gallery, London: 110
Carola Oman, *Nelson* (London 1946): 28, 138, 139
Collections of the Ruling Prince of Liechtenstein, Vaduz: 13, 59

Map (162) from the Atlas of British History
All other illustrations from the picture archive of the Austrian National Library.

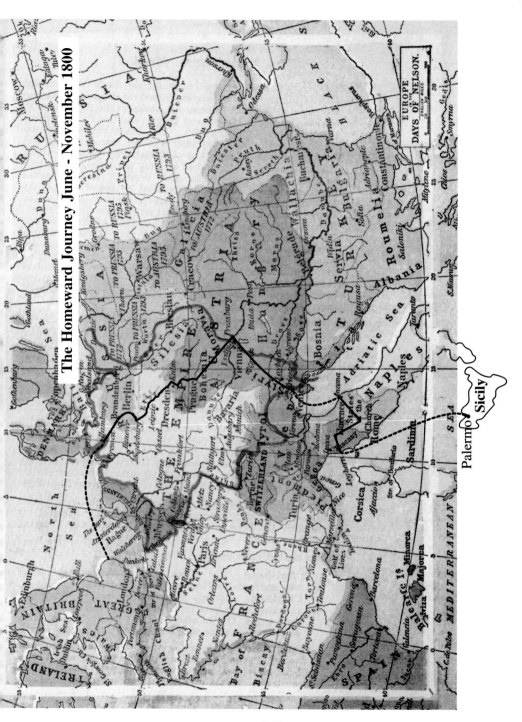

The Homeward Journey June - November 1800

EUROPE
IN THE
DAYS OF NELSON.

Palermo
Sicily

# The Homeward Journey

## Year 1800

## Chronology

| | | |
|---|---|---|
| 10 June | Palermo | Queen Maria Carolina, son, three daughters, royal party and the Hamiltons sail on *Foudroyant* and *Alexander* in company with four Russian ships and an English frigate. |
| 14 June | Livorno (Leghorn) | Arrived. Nelson shifts flag from *Foudroyant* to *Alexander* and strikes flag 11 July. |
| 12 July | Florence | Royal party leaves 14 July and Nelson and Hamiltons on the 16 following route via Arezzo and Foligno to Ancona. |
| 24 July | Ancona | Both parties reunited and board vessels of a Russian Squadron for the voyage to Trieste. |
| 1 August | Trieste | Arrived and onward departure delayed through illness of party members. Queen's party sets off for Vienna followed two days later by Nelson's party. |
| 13/15 August | Graz | |
| 18 August-<br>26 September | Vienna | Arrived for stay of five and a half weeks. Queen Maria Carolina and party remain in Vienna. |
| 27 September | Prague | Arrived. Nelson's birthday celebrated 29 September. Departed 30 September embarking at Lobositz on River Elbe. |
| 2-10 October | Dresden | Arrived and re-embarked on River Elbe for Magdeburg on 10 October. |
| 15 October | Magdeburg | Arrived and resumed river passage to Hamburg 15 October. |
| 21 October | Hamburg | Arrived. |
| 31 October | | Sailed on mail packet *King George,* hired by Nelson, for Great Yarmouth. |
| 6 November | Gt. Yarmouth | Arrived. Nelson granted Freedom of the Borough of Great Yarmouth. |
| 8 November | London | Completion of journey and reunited with Lady Nelson and Revd. Edmund Nelson. |

# THE NELSON SOCIETY
## PRESIDENT – The Rt. Hon. The Earl Nelson

The Nelson Society was inaugurated in Norwich in 1981, and the Constitution of the Society defines the objects of the Society thus:

"to advance public education in the appreciation of the character and life of Admiral Lord Nelson and in furtherance of this aim to arrange: talks, meetings, seminars and lectures, visits and expeditions, the publication of books and papers, journals and other material and to do all other lawful things as are necessary for the attainment of these objects."

The Nelson Society is thus approaching its twentieth anniversary and has reason to be pleased with progress, although there is much to be done to fulfil all the objects laid down by our Founders.

Thanks are due to the members and Committee of The Nelson Society for their continuing support, which has made this progress possible, and with whom we move forward through the 'Nelson Decade', commemorating the bicentenary of Nelson's greatest achievements, which will culminate with the 200th anniversary of Trafalgar in 2005.

e-mail nelson.society@rjt.co.uk
websites http://www.nelson-society.org.uk
http://board.to/topsail

# INDEX